dead orthodoxy or living heresy?

p andrew sandlin

K

KERYGMA
PRESS

LA GRANGE, CALIFORNIA

Primitive Truths for Postmodern Times

Kerygma Press
P. O. Box 415
Mount Hermon, California 95041
www.christianculture.com

Kerygma Press is the theological imprint of the Center for Cultural Leadership.
CCL is a non-profit Christian educational foundation devoted to influencing
Christians for effective cultural leadership — in church, the arts, education, business,
technology, science, and other realms of contemporary culture

Printed in the United States of America

ISBN 978-0-578-00001-5

To

Peace

Who has turned out to be quite a tempest.

Table of Contents

Preface

This book is a collection of lectures, talks and sermons I've delivered over the last five years. I've left them in the substantial format in which I first uttered them. Therefore, they lack the stylistic elements of a communication originally intended to be read, not heard. I hope that they'll compensate in content for what they lack in polish. I've added footnotes to show where I've gotten many of my ideas, but I could never list — or remember — all of the sources on which I have relied. As I get older it seems that my own ideas so mesh with the ideas of those to whom I am indebted for them that I despair to separate whose ideas are whose, though no one else should be blamed for my own mistaken ideas.

I write amid uniquely troubled times for Christianity in the West. Throughout history, the Christian church has been assailed by foes on many fronts, including heretics within its midst. Not until the last 100 years, however, has the church in the West suffered from comprehensive frontal treachery — I refer to theological liberals, who have wished to remain *within* the church while denying the very heart of the Faith.[1] To compound matters, in the last few decades, this liberalism has even infested conservative ranks known as evangelicalism.[2] Today, one may deny the authority of the Bible,[3] the substitutionary death of Jesus Christ,[4] and the omniscience and omnipotence of God Almighty[5] and still be called an evangelical. What has changed is not the fact of the assaults on the Faith but

---

1. Donald E. Miller, *The Case for Liberal Christianity* (San Francisco: Harper & Row, 1981).
2. Millard J. Erickson, *The Evangelical Left* (Grand Rapids: Baker, 1997); cf., Gary Dorrien, *The Remaking of Evangelical Theology* (Louisville, Kentucky, John Knox, 1998).
3. Brian D. McLaren, *A Generous Orthodoxy* (Grand Rapids: Zondervan, 2004), 171. To be truly Biblical, McLaren suggests, is not to look to the Bible as an "encyclopedia of timeless moral truths" but rather ascertain how the Bible inspires Christians today to be His people in the present and future. The array of New Testament speakers and writers who cited the Old Testament precisely as though it contains "timeless moral truths" would beg to differ.
4. Dave Tomlinson, *The Post-Conservative Evangelical* (El Cajon, California: EmergentYS, 2003), 100-102.
5. Clark H. Pinnock, *Most Moved Mover* (Carlisle, Cumbria, England: Paternoster, 2001).

rather their *locus* — today those assaults repose in the throne-room of evangelical Christianity, "the new Christianity in the old church."[6] The converse movement in some of the mainline denominations toward a more historically orthodox Faith,[7] while most laudable, cannot compensate for the wholesale sell-out of Biblical, apostolic Christianity in the very places that trumpet fidelity to it. It should come as no surprise that moral decline in the surrounding culture, at one time pervasively, if imperfectly, Christian, has followed the sell-out of the Faith in the churches.[8]

It's my considered conviction that the only antidote to this ecclesial and cultural apostasy is the recovery of a full-orbed, Spirit-drenched, intellectually rigorous Biblical Faith, devoted to classical Christianity (ancient catholic orthodoxy); attentive, but not slavishly committed to, the Reformation-era confessions; and marinated in a love for God, for the saints, and for the world. I write from the standpoint of an older Reformational evangelicalism, and underlying the disparate addresses of this book is the conviction that Jesus Christ is Lord of all life and that no area of thought and culture is exempt from His authority.[9]

The sequence of this book is as follows: Chapter 1 is a sermon preached at Church of the King-Santa Cruz on the 25th anniversary of my first ordination. Chapter 2 was delivered several times at the Blackstone School of Law, sponsored by the Alliance Defense Fund. Chapter 3 comprises an opening statement at the Roman Catholic-Evangelical Dialogue held in Chicago under the auspices of both ACT 3 and the Center for Cultural Leadership.

---

6. G. C. Berkouwer, *Modern Uncertainty and Christian Faith* (Grand Rapids: Eerdmans, 1953), 29.
7. Thomas C. Oden, *Turning Around the Mainline* (Grand Rapids: Baker, 2006).
8. Christopher Dawson, *The Making of Europe* (London: Sheed & Ward, 1948).
9. *E.g.*, Abraham Kuyper, *Principles of Sacred Theology* (Grand Rapids: Baker, 1898, 1980); Benjamin Breckinridge Warfield, "Calvinism," *Calvin and Augustine* (Philadelphia: Presbyterian and Reformed, 1956), ch. 5; Carl F. H. Henry, *Evangelical Responsibility in Contemporary Theology* (Grand Rapids: Eerdmans, 1957); Cornelius Van Til, *An Introduction to Systematic Theology* (Phillipsburg, New Jersey: Presbyterian and Reformed, 1974, 1982); Donald Bloesch, *Essentials of Evangelical Theology* (San Francisco: Harper & Row, 1978-1979); and Francis A. Schaeffer, *The Complete Works of Francis A. Schaeffer* (Westchester, Illinois: Crossway, 1982), five vols.

Chapter 4 is a graduation address delivered at Edinburg Theological Seminary, Edinburg, Texas. I preached Chapter 5 at Church of the King-Santa Cruz in a series on the book of 1 Corinthians, just as I preached Chapter 6 in my exposition of the book of Romans. Chapter 7 was originally intended to appear in my book *Un-Inventing the Church: Toward a Modest Ecclesiology* and was delivered more informally as a sermon on several occasions. Chapter 8 is the text of the commencement address delivered at Annapolis Christian Academy, Corpus Christi, Texas. I delivered Chapter 9 at a conference on Christian education of the Southern California Center for Christian Studies in Newport Beach, California. Finally, chapter 10 was a talk given at the Family Advance at the Trinity Presbyterian Church in Valparaiso, Florida. I am thankful for all of the invitations that made these addresses possible and for the patience and attentiveness of every audience to which I spoke.

I am grateful to Matt Mazerik for carefully proofreading the entire manuscript. His suggestions were invaluable, but I alone am responsible for residual errors.

P. Andrew Sandlin
August, 2008

CHAPTER 1

The Old-Time Religion
is (Still) Good Enough for Me

*Dedicated to my Father and Mother, from whom I first
learned "The Old-Time Religion"*

Recently my wife Sharon and I were reframing my diplomas
and certificates, and I noticed something I'd forgotten: The
first Sunday of January in 1983 was the date of my first ordination
to the Gospel ministry. I have two ordinations, one Baptist and
one as Reformed, and I'm proud of and identify with both.

I've been preaching since I was 16 years old, but twenty-five
years ago today I formally started my Gospel ministry.

It's been quite a ride.

I hope you'll indulge me this morning as I reflect on the old-
time religion, the great old Faith that my parents first taught me.
The great old Faith to which I (and this church, by the way) am
formally committed. The great old Faith that this sinful world
desperately needs.

You've heard the quaint old song, "The Old Time Religion":
"It was good enough for Paul and Peter and my father and mother
and it's good enough for me." A simple old song, but like a lot of
simple old songs, it conveys the truth more effectively than some
complex songs. "The Old Time Religion" is an ancient landmark
that my father — and our fathers — have set.

I intend that it not be removed. Not on my watch.

No, I'm happy and privileged and proud to carry on "The
Old Time Religion."

I don't mean that every old thing is good and every new
thing is bad. That's a silly, reactionary credo. We need to get
rid of lots of old things, and we need to adopt lots of new things.
After all, aren't we happy for microwaves and automobiles and

freeways and anesthetic? The same is true in the Christian Faith. I'm glad for the Eastern Church's contribution to Trinitarianism. I'm glad for the Western church's contribution to Christian culture. I'm glad for the Reformation view of justification by faith alone (which represented a break with the [recent] past). I'm glad for the Wesleyan view of revival. And a lot of other comparatively newer things, too. We have to be willing to adopt new things — even new views — when they are the right things and right views. We must be willing to change.

Over these 25 years, I've changed my mind on a lot of things.

Years ago as a young preacher I heard an older minister trumpet from the pulpit, apparently with a great deal of pride, "I haven't changed one of my doctrinal beliefs in 40 years of my ministry."

I knew when I heard him that the man was either a fool or a liar. Any Christian minister so inflexible in all his beliefs as to refuse to change even one in the face of the experience and illumination of 40 years is a fool, and if he did change his mind but asserted that he has not changed, he is a liar.

New things can be good things. Compared to the Pharisees' tradition, Jesus' message was a new message. He said so (Mt. 9:14-17). The Gospel was new at one time — the new religion within the collapsing ancient Roman Empire. It was replacing the old pagan polytheistic religions.

But "The Old-Time Religion" does have specific and valid meaning. Most of Western Europe was formally Christian until about 150 years ago. Christians disagreed among themselves — but they agreed on the main things, the things we confess in the great old creeds. They believed in Jesus' blood atonement and in His resurrection and in the Bible as the Word of God.

They believed "The Old-Time Religion."

As a result of the Enlightenment and other factors, all that has changed. We live in a highly secular world that practices a new religion: the religion of humanism. Man as the center and measure of all things. Even many of the churches have a "Christianized" version of this humanism, religious liberalism. It's not the great old Faith. It's a new faith and the wrong faith.

"The Old-Time Religion" and the Gospel

"The Old-Time Religion," by contrast, centers in Jesus. His early apostles preached it. What is it? That Jesus is the Son of God. He died for our sins on the Cross of Calvary. He died in our place: "substitutionary atonement." He paid the penalty for our sins.[1] He rose bodily from the grave to defeat the power of sin. He beat down the Devil's power when He rose from the dead.[2] He's alive with the Father today, ruling and reigning and interceding for us, His followers. One day He'll come back to earth just as He left.[3] Then He'll get rid of all sin and set everything right.

We belong to Jesus and gain eternal life by trusting in Him, and not in ourselves. By faith, we can have all our sins forgiven and be made a child of the King. Not by our works, but by His faithful death on the Cross and His resurrection.

This is the Gospel, the Good News (see chapter 3). That Jesus is Savior and Lord. All who own Him as Lord and Savior will be His children forever. He'll forgive them and clean them up and in cleaning them up, He'll clean up the world of its sin.

So often our hymns are better than our theology: "What can wash away my sin? Nothing but the blood of Jesus. What can make me whole again? Nothing but the blood of Jesus." "There is a fountain filed with blood drawn from Immanuel's veins, and sinners plunged beneath that flood lose all their guilty stains." These hymns communicate more Biblical truth, and they communicate it more succinctly and effectively, than most sermons preached today.

---

1. Leon Morris, *The Apostolic Preaching of the Cross* (Grand Rapids: Eerdmans, 1955, 1960).

2. Oscar Cullmann, "Immortality of the Soul or Resurrection of the Dead: The Witness of the New Testament," in ed., Krester Stendahl, *Immortality and Resurrection* (New York: The Macmillan Company, 1965), 9-53.

3. It's tragic that on the one hand we have Christians who attach the most obsessive, fantastic interpretations to the Second Coming of Jesus while others, in reaction, are embarrassed by the Second Coming and refuse to talk about it. But the Second Coming is a fundamental doctrine of the Bible, and to be embarrassed over the Second Coming is just as apostate as to be embarrassed over the bodily resurrection of Jesus. The primitive church was an *eschatological* community. See James D. G. Dunn, *Unity and Diversity in the New Testament* (London: SCM Press, 2006, third edition), 13-16.

This is "The Old-Time Religion." The old-time Gospel of
the apostles and of Paul and the other early Christians. It's the
ancient landmark message.[4]

And if we lose that message, *we have lost everything.*

Attacks on the old-time Gospel abound. We all know about
theological liberalism. It's the idea that Christianity has to be
changed to fit in with the current age. If that means that resurrection from the dead is not believable, then let's throw it away.
If the modern age finds blood atonement incredible, let's trash
it. Gresham Machen was right. Whatever this is, it's not the
Christian Faith.[5] Liberalism is a different religion, a false religion,
a Luciferian religion. I refer to all the churches in California (and
elsewhere) that believe Jesus was just a man. That He never rose
bodily from the grave. That good works can save you, by being
politically correct (protecting the spotted owl). What self-righteous
rubbish! This is the religion of man, not of God. And it sends
people to Hell.

This attack is even launched by evangelicals. Some of them
are saying that the Cross — the substitutionary atonement — is
"cosmic child abuse."[6] What blasphemy! God deliver us from the
attacks on the Cross.

And there will never be Gospel success apart from the mighty,
onrushing power of the Holy Spirit that we see in the primitive
church. The Holy Spirit in the Risen Christ supplies the power to
the Christian church and life, but Christians are too often afraid
of the Holy Spirit's power. They ignore it. They poke run at Holy
Spirit revival. They even hold conferences against revival. Well,
good riddance to them. There will be no great Gospel success apart
from the power of the Spirit, and we won't have it as long as we
make fun of it and refuse to cry out to God for that precious power

4. H. N. Ridderbos, "The General Character of Paul's Preaching of Christ," *Paul and Jesus* (Nutley, New Jersey: Presbyterian and Reformed, 1977), 74-79 and "The Redemptive-Historical Character of Paul's Preaching," *When the Time Had Fully Come* (Jordan Station, Ontario, Canada, 1957, 1982), 74-79.
5. J. Gresham Machen, *Christianity and Liberalism* (Grand Rapids: Eerdmans, 1933).
6. Steve Jeffery, Michael Ovey and Andrew Sach, *Pierced for Our Transgressions* (Wheaton, Illinois: Crossway, 2007), 228-233.

(see chapter 7).

That power is a big part of "The Old-Time Religion."

"The Old-Time Religion" and the Bible

Where do we learn about "The Old-Time Religion"? An old-time Book, the Bible. The Bible is the Word of God. Men wrote it, but God inspired them. He mysteriously guided them in such a way that what they wrote was His revelation to man.[7]

If we don't have the Bible, we don't know about Jesus and the Gospel. Revelation in creation is glorious, but it doesn't give us the Gospel. Only the Bible gives us a definitive, authoritative account of the Gospel.

This is what makes the Bible so valuable. It's the record of the message of the apostles about what Jesus has done for us and for the world. There can be no salvation without that knowledge. So, if we don't have the apostolic record, their witness, we cannot be saved. There's no other way of knowing.

But the Bible is more than the apostles' witness. It is the very living Word of the living God. It tells us what God wants us to know. We are not left in the dark by a hidden God. We are not straining to hear a mute God. God has spoken. What a miracle![8]

This Word is your and my food. It sustains us in the frequently parched spiritual desert into which we wonder (Jer. 15:16). It's a lamp to our feet and a light to our path (Ps. 119:105). We live in a dark place sometimes — not just the evil world around us, but the confusion that clouds our sinful, finite minds. We need the light. We need to know how to live.

Recently this happened to me. "God, I don't understand what you're doing." So I turned to the Word, and it en*light*ened me.

I'm not a fundamentalist or a liberal. The fundamentalist

---

7. There can be no doubt that this is the very old-time view of the very earliest Christians. See George Duncan Berry, *The Inspiration and Authority of Holy Scripture* (London: Society for Promoting Christian Knowledge, 1919), 28.
8. G. C. Berkouwer, *Modern Uncertainty and Christian Faith* (Grand Rapids: Eerdmans, 1953), 18-24.

faith is too narrow and truncated.[9] The liberal faith is … well, it's not a faith; actually, it's faith in man. It's a false religion.

But if I had to choose between the two, I'd have to be a fundamentalist. At least the fundamentalist believes the Bible and Jesus. At least the fundamentalist is in touch with the Gospel. Liberals are not.

The Bible has been under attack for 200 years, but today it's attacked even in putative evangelical churches. "The Bible is not reliable in historical matters," or "The Bible presents an outmoded picture of ethics," or, "The Bible is meant merely to inspire us, not to govern our lives."

I decided a long time ago that if I am to follow Jesus, I must have no lower view of the Bible than my Lord did. He had the Old Testament. How did He treat it? As the very living Word of God. Not once did He cast doubt on it. Not once did He question its historical accounts. Not once did our Lord waver about its total veracity. Jesus Christ treated the Old Testament as the very inspired Word of God.

If I'm to follow Him, can I have any view lower than He did?[10]

Of course, we could always say that Jesus was wrong about the Old Testament.

But then we'd have an even greater problem.

If we are to be Christians, followers of Jesus, we must hold the same view of the Scriptures He did. And that means the infallible, inspired Word of God.

That's "The Old-Time Religion."

"The Old-Time Religion" and Lordship

Finally, "The Old-Time Religion" is all about the earliest creed of the church: "Jesus is Lord." The chief *doctrine* of the

---

9. Carl F. H. Henry, *The Uneasy Conscience of Modern Fundamentalism* (Grand Rapids: Eerdmans, 1947).

10. Clark H. Pinnock, "The Inspiration of Scripture and the Authority of Jesus Christ," in ed., John Warwick Montgomery, *God's Inerrant Word* (Minneapolis, Minnesota: Bethany, 1974), 201-218.

Bible is the resurrection of Jesus. The leading *message* of the Bible is the Gospel of Jesus. But the overarching *theme* of the Bible is the Lordship of Jesus.[11]

The primitive Christians understood this, and so should we (see chapter 4). They gave their lives — many of them — for the Risen Lord. We should be willing to do the same.

Jesus is Lord of the *individual* — everyone, but particularly Christians. It starts when we get saved. We trust in Jesus by faith, and we give our life to Him.

I talked a few minutes ago about the perversion of liberalism, turning salvation into a human-performance plan. But there's another perversion: denying Jesus' Lordship in salvation. He saves us by His grace, but not without our submission. Jesus died not just to take us to Heaven but also to make us disciples, and if we are not His disciples, we have no part in Him.

And Jesus is Lord of the *family*. He doesn't deal just with individuals as individuals. He deals with families as families. The wife is to join with the husband in following Jesus. He calls the entire family to follow Him. You children are not your own; you belong to Jesus. You are an offering to Him. That's why you are baptized. That's why you eat the communion meal. You are part of His community. And you are called to follow Him all the days of your life.

Jesus is Lord of the *church*. The church is the visible covenant community. All those who profess faith in Jesus and are baptized along with their children. The church confesses, "Jesus is Lord." The church is God's kingdom outpost in the world. The church confesses, "Let Jesus be Lord on earth as He is Lord in Heaven."

The church is not the Lord. Too many of today's "high-churchmen" had better learn that lesson. The church testifies to the Lord, but the church is not the Lord. Being baptized doesn't save you. The elders aren't dispensers of salvation. The minister is not "the voice of Jesus," and other such sacrilege. Jesus is Lord of His church, and you and I are *not* Lord.

---

11 A. W. Tozer's *The Best of A. W. Tozer* (Harrisburg, Pennsylvania: Christian Publications, 1978).

The church is called to preserve and expand "The Old-Time Religion." In the striking phrase of Chuck Colson, the church is "the community of memory."[12] In a world of spiritual amnesiacs, a world of fads and trends and continuous transformations, the church is charged with perpetuating the old, old truths of the Gospel, the Bible and the Lordship of Jesus. That's why we're here: to keep it going. And to get others to keep it going. Jesus is Lord of the church.

And Jesus is Lord of the *culture*.[13] The idea that Jesus is Lord of our private lives and families and the church but not Lord of business and wealth and economics and technology and science is a silly old wives' tale that has sold today's church into slavery. If Jesus is Lord at all, He's Lord of everything, and our job is to press His claims in the office and on the showroom floor and in the voting booth and the laboratory and out on the Pacific waves and everywhere else. There is religiously no neutral ground. Religious neutrality is a myth, and our goal is to explode that myth by being public Christians, not just private Christians.

Concluding: "The Old-Time Religion" is not a matter of intellectual assent. When the great tsunamis of life arrive and crash onto the serene shore of your life and mine, "intellectual assent" just won't cut it. You had better have a heart given wholly to God. A life that knows how to do business with God — to pray to God and hear from Him and live before Him in passion. Children, you need more than your parents' instruction; you need your parents' God.

Ideas (vital though they are) do not rule the world. Passions rule the world, and our passion for God should rule us and the world.

That's "The Old-Time Religion." It's been good enough for me for many years.

I pray that it's good enough for you.

---

12. Charles Colson, "Community of Memory," *Christianity Today* on-line, http://www.christianitytoday.com/ct/2007/october/36.156.html, October 15, 2007.
13. Francis A. Schaeffer, *The Complete Works of Francis A. Schaeffer* (Westchester, Illinois: Crossway, 1982), five vols.

CHAPTER 2

Dead Orthodoxy or Living Heresy?

There is so little orthodoxy of any kind today, it would be refreshing to find even some dead orthodoxy.

Gordon H. Clark, *In Defense of Theology*[1]

A Spiritual Aristocracy

Let's not mince words here under the guise of pious modesty. While elitism is often a bad thing, it is probably fair to say that you students at the Blackstone School of Law constitute a Christian elite — better yet, a "spiritual aristocracy." We're all saved by grace, and therefore there's no room to boast before either God *or* man, but we must squarely face the fact that you are a spiritual aristocracy. The legal profession wields great influence — both for good and ill — in contemporary culture. As well-educated Christian attorneys, you are being charged not merely to be both good Christians and good attorneys, but to act "Christianly" in the jurisprudential profession. The goal (again, let's not mince words) is the re-Christianization of law. In other words, to rigorously apply the truth of Christianity in the legal profession. But, even this gargantuan task is not enough. You must not merely apply the truth; you must *incarnate* that truth. Talk about responsibility! With much giftedness goes much responsibility — you are called to incarnate the truth with which you've been gifted.

Incarnational Truth

Unfortunately, the Western tradition, even significant portions of the Christian tradition, has been indifferent or even ac-

---

1. Milford, Michigan: Mott Media, 1984), 12, n. 2.

tively hostile to an incarnational approach to truth. As Lesslie Newbigin has suggested, we have inherited from Greco-Roman thinking the notion that theory and practice constitute chief distinctions of life.[2] Theory first employs our bare reason to erect an ideational architecture, and then, when all is rationally tidy, we attempt to put it into practice.

This Greco-Roman model is quite different from the Hebraic-Biblical approach. According to the Hebrews and to Jesus and His apostles, life is about *faith and obedience* (two sides of the same coin), and not theory and practice. Jesus Himself declared to His disciples that those who follow the will of the Father *will* know of His doctrine (Jn. 7:17). In other words, we gain knowledge as we obey; we do not create some sort of architectonic rational system and then attempt to implement it. We are called to obey the voice of Jesus and His Word, and in obeying, we will learn the truth. Let's explore this issue for a moment.

The Western philosophical tradition from Descartes down to Hegel and Kant is largely interested in epistemology — the source and nature of knowledge. How does man know, and what does he know? This tradition was much less interested in what we today term ontology — the study of being, particularly man's being. The reaction to this obsession with epistemology set in with Søren Kierkegaard and late 19th and early 20th century existentialists like Nietzsche and Heidegger. Apart from Kierkegaard, this existentialism was largely non-Christian, and often anti-Christian, but it was surely correct in drawing the emphasis away from epistemology and concentrating on ontology (see chapter 8).

For too long, Christians have aped the rationalism (or, for that matter, empiricism) of the Western tradition and have been obsessed with *knowing* rather than *being*. This has things just backwards. Jesus wants us to be who we should be; then we will know what we should know! Salvation is not merely a change of mind, as though we simply need to assimilate a few new ideas. No, according to Jesus in his statement to Nicodemus recorded in John

---

2. Lesslie Newbigin, *Proper Confidence* (Grand Rapids: Eerdmans, 1995), 38.

3, an individual must be "born again," or born from above. God must give him new dispositions, a new heart. He must become a new creation (2 Cor. 5:17). He doesn't need merely a mind change; he needs a *nature* change. And when his nature changes, his mind will (incrementally) change.

These sentiments are not often appealing to smart people like us, because, aware of the power of ideas, we somehow think that individual transformation is mostly a rational affair. But it is not. Reason is simply one component among many, and sometimes it is not even the main one.

Let me probe even a little more uncomfortably. We cannot expect to change jurisprudence or the culture of the world until we change *ourselves*. On this point, Gandhi was correct: "Be the change you want to see in the world." Of course, I am not implying that man has it within his power to effect life-changes. God works in us to do His good will and pleasure, and yet, He tells us to work out our own salvation with fear and trembling (Phil. 2:10). Turn us, says the prophet, and we will be turned (Lam. 5:21). And yet Jehovah declared curtly to His apostate people: "Get a new heart" (Ezek. 18:31). God's providence is no excuse for human irresponsibility. *We cannot become agents for godly change until we ourselves have been sufficiently changed.*

It's imperative to recognize that we are not undiluted conduits of objective truth. While Kierkegaard was wrong when he declared, "Truth is subjectivity," he would have been right had he declared, "Truth is *meshed* in subjectivity." Similarly, in the words of Eric Hoffer:

> The wisdom of others remains dull till it is writ over with our own blood. We are essentially apart from the world; it bursts into our consciousness only when it sinks its teeth and nails into us.[3]

The idea-only men and women "are essentially apart from the world." There is no Christian efficacy, no cultural leadership,

---

3. Eric Hoffer, *The Passionate State of Mind* (New York, 1954), 115.

in the future of these men and women. Cultural leaders are individuals into whom the truth "sinks its teeth and nails." It consumes them. It does not consume their intellect. It consumes their
very being.

The truth should bear heavily on our souls. In a concrete
sense, *the Faith is what we are.* I know a scholar, a gifted thinker
and proficient writer, who champions authentic Christian theology; however, when that theology comes out of his fingertips onto
the keyboard, it is a distorted, vindictive, insulting, uncharitable
theology. Why is this? Because he is a distorted, vindictive, insulting man. The man is shaped by the theology, true enough, but
the theology is also shaped by the man. The same is true in any
profession, including the jurisprudential profession. Weak, vacillating, and undisciplined attorneys produce weak, vacillating, and
undisciplined jurisprudence. Remember this. Truth is always objective, but truth is never *only* objective. It is held hostage to the
virtue, vices, sleights, ambitions, flaws, sins, and passions of the
individuals who encounter it.[4]

Ideas: Necessary, But Never Sufficient

Just after World War II, at the nadir of conservative influence,
Richard Weaver wrote a significant book, *Ideas Have Consequences.*[5]
It was a boon to conservatives. Following Edmund Burke, they
had usually rested their case on precept and precedent (like good
legal experts do), and less on discursive reasoning.[6] Conservatives
didn't have a lot of new ideas; they didn't *need* new ideas. In fact,
that was the problem with liberals — obsession with new ideas.
So, when Weaver and others showed up with ideational defenses
of conservatism, the intellectually adept conservatives jumped in

---

4. Situating the consideration of ontology (being) prior to other specific philosophical
(and theological) issues — particularly epistemology (knowledge) — was rightly the
unique sequence of Martin Heidegger. See George Steiner, *Martin Heidegger* (Chicago:
University of Chicago, 1978, 1989), 19-20. Reformed apologist Cornelius Van Til
articulated this sequence from a distinctly Christian perspective. See e.g., n. 9 below.
5. (Chicago: University of Chicago, 1948).
6. Russell Kirk, *The Conservative Mind* (Chicago: Henry Regnery, 1953), ch. 2.

with both feet. This trend affected even Christian conservatives, especially those susceptible to ideologies (an ideology is a highly structured, generally comprehensive view of reality). These guys liked it all figured out rationally; "We need 'The System' to get it done culturally." And so they spent all sorts of intellectual and emotional capital to devise the system that would get our culture back on the right track.

The problem is that some of these same folks had massive personal problems — vindictiveness, pride, avarice, anger, fornication, lack of forgiveness, and so on. And as always, their deeply flawed ontology (and here I'm not suggesting that sin is metaphysical; I'm just speaking loosely) — their deeply flawed ontology shaped their ideas. In other words, they imported some of themselves into "The System."

This is inescapable. And it should sober you and me. We do not deliver an objective system. *We deliver ourselves.* When you deliver briefs, you deliver yourself. When you deliver scholarly papers, you deliver yourself. When you deliver lectures, you deliver yourself. When you deliver books, you deliver yourself. When you deliver programs for cultural reclamation, you deliver yourself.

Let us not allow our commitment to objective truth to exempt us from the painful but brave decisions we must make in particular historical situations. And know this — ethics must be relevant to particular historical situations. There are grave errors to avoid here. One: fighting yesterday's battles today. There are so many examples I could adduce. I'll give just a couple. The battle between orthodox denominations should be a thing of the past. We don't need orthodox Catholics and Protestants fighting one another to the death.[7] Let's get out of the 16th century. Another: the Enlightenment battle for rational objectivity. Descartes and his Enlightenment cohorts were convinced that reason is objective, somehow detached from the person *in toto*, and could operate virtually independently. So, they tended over time to battle faith and superstition with "reason," with faith itself being the most

7. Thomas Oden, *The Rebirth of Orthodoxy* (New York: HarperCollins, 2003).

egregious form of superstition.[8] While reason is a vital instrument in perceiving truth, the Christian view is that truth in one of its supreme forms is incarnational; the Logos is a Person, not chiefly a principle (Jn. 1:1-3). The pure objectivity of reason is perhaps the most superstitious faith of all, because it does not account for man's spiritual condition, which shapes his reason. The battle is never between faith and reason, *but always between rival faiths.* Let's not imitate the errors of our forebears, who vested unaided reason with some sort of kingly objectivity and invited the non-Christians to reason on that basis.[9] Let us ask them to submit to the One through whom *alone* all things — including reason — make sense.

We cannot live in the past.

So, then, before we set the agenda for changing the culture, let us set the agenda for changing *ourselves.* Are we, in fact, truly Jesus' disciples, having submitted ourselves to His Lordship? Do we beseech God to be filled with His Spirit, knowing that apart from the filling of the Spirit, all of our efforts (and not only our jurisprudential efforts) will be ineffectual? Are we Christians who equally value charity and truth or, better yet, the truth of charity and the charity of truth? Or do we, on the one hand, compromise clear Biblical truth to get along with a depraved postmodern world? Or, on the other hand, do we compromise love in our zeal to be right (including theologically right) at all costs? Do we recognize the *equal* error of these sins? Are we more interested in being successful attorneys than of being successful Christians, recognizing, however, that the only authentically successful attorneys *are* successful Christians? Are we humble Christians, or are we proud of our own precise doctrinal system, our own unique experiences, our own stellar church and denomination? Do we revel in provincialism and sectarianism, quite sure that our expression of the Christian Faith is so far superior to everybody else's that we needn't trifle with them? Are we committed to Biblical ethics, including personal ethics, such that we are willing to swear to our

8. Peter Gay, *Age of Enlightenment* (New York, Time, 1966).
9. Cornelius Van Til, *A Survey of Christian Epistemology* (Phillipsburg, New Jersey: Presbyterian and Reformed, n.d).

own hurt (Ps. 15:4), rather than breach Christian and legal ethics? Are we interested only in making lots of money (though there is nothing wrong with making lots of money), and not in moving forward in sanctification? Most significantly, do our hearts burn with a passion to love God and His Son, Jesus, with all of our heart, soul, mind, and might? Are we willing, in a genuine, reflective sense, to be "Jesus freaks"?

These are the sorts of questions with which we must honestly confront ourselves, and that we must honestly answer. It will not suffice merely to secure the right sources, procure the right knowledge, and proffer the right answers — even if they are Christian sources, knowledge, and answers. We must not be merely hearers of the Word, but also doers. Faith without works is dead, James tells us in chapter 2 of his epistle.

We must be vigilant in maintaining the proper relation between faith and works. When we see Christianity as only an objective Faith, supplied with theological truth content, we become arid Christians and churches — truly a "dead orthodoxy." Conversely, when truth and its theological identity no longer matter, but what really matters is only our personal experience of joy and hope, we are susceptible to grave error — living heresy. But we are called *neither* to dead orthodoxy *nor* to living heresy — we are called to living orthodoxy! The orthodox Trinity is not primarily a paradigm for speculation, but a practice for spirituality.

Do we daily look to God as our Father, mediated by the redemptive work of the Son, Jesus Christ, and the filling and power of the Holy Spirit? The Lordship of Jesus Christ, the prime message of the New Testament, is not simply a pleasant sounding phrase; it should immerse our lives.

Do we first ask ourselves, "What does the Lord require?" Do we train our covenant children in the nurture and admonition of the Lord? Do we treat our wife as Christ does His Church, loving and cherishing, and, if necessary, sacrificing our lives for her? Do we study and practice law to the glory of God? Do we look at God's revelation in the Bible and in creation for the absolutes on which we erect systems of human jurisprudence? Do we speak prophetically against the pernicious ideologies of our age — post-modernism, feminism, machismo, evolutionism, materialism (both philosophical and practical), socialism, sociological and utilitarian jurisprudence, and so on? We are not called first of all to accomplish *something*. We are called first of all to *be* something. We are called to *be* God's people.

Nor may we underestimate the truth content of Sacred Scripture, particularly as it comes to the fore in ancient catholic orthodoxy shaped by ecclesiastical consensus around which all Christians joyfully close rank. We stand uncompromisingly for the Triune God, Jesus Christ as fully God and fully Man, creation *ex nihilo*, Jesus' atoning death and bodily resurrection and Second Coming; the reality of the Church, the communion of the saints, and the forgiveness of sin, and so forth. It is *this* orthodoxy, not merely a political conservatism, that must meet the challenges of secularism, and its social depravities — elective abortion, homosexual "marriage," pornography, "value-free" education, euthanasia, no-fault divorce, and other social blights. *This* Christian orthodoxy will equally meet the challenge of twisted Fundamentalisms like Islamo-fascism.[10] It is *this* orthodoxy, and not a vague commitment to "democratic values" (though we surely appreciate the benefits of democracy) that will stand as a bulwark against the social evils that confront us.

Finally, this orthodoxy, properly understood, sheds sectarianism, which threatens a catholicity calling Christians to work together for a Christian culture — a Christian culture, I say, not a Protestant culture or a Roman Catholic culture or an Eastern Orthodox culture or a Baptist culture or a Calvinist culture or a Pentecostal culture or anything else. We can — and should — maintain our strong theological and ecclesiastical distinctives while joining hands for a *Christian* culture anchored squarely in ancient catholic orthodoxy, which we all hold in common. This is the burning need of the hour, and it is a need that must be addressed by the right *kind* of Christian.

---

10. Bernard Lewis, *The Crisis of Islam* (New York: Random House, 2003).

This Christian must know God, not merely *about* God. He and she must know the Bible — all of it, not just his or her pet verses. He must know the history of Christianity, of Western civilization, of the church, of theology. He must know the times in which we live. He must know himself. He must know his cultural enemies.

Knowing and Being

But he must not only *know*. Fundamentally, he must *be*. Knowing springs from *being*. He must be God-intoxicated.[11] He must be consumed with the Faith. He must be a leader, not only of individuals, but also of culture. He must, therefore, be culturally astute, aware of his crucial role during a particular historical period. He must be intelligent. He must be a visionary, a futurist, a risk-taker, a dynamist.[12] He must be open to new and unique ways of thinking and acting that further the orthodox, Christian Faith. He must be urgent, direct, self-assured, virtuous, persevering. He must be holy without being pharisaic. He must be pious without being pietistic. He must be confident without being cocky. He must be self-sacrificial without being self-deprecating. He must be independent without being contemptuous. He must be bold without being insulting. He must be this-worldly without being worldly. He must persevere through criticism and adversity. He must lead both by idea and example. He must be a man of God who is not less a man of this world because he is a man of God, and in fact, a man of this world precisely because he *is* a man of God.

This man and woman must be more than godly. *He must be able to communicate and disseminate this godliness throughout a culture.* He must not be content with his own belief in and practice of Christianity. He must desire the Christianization of all of society. Further, he must prepare himself for his task by cultivating those

11. A. W. Tozer, *The Pursuit of God* (Camp Hill, Pennsylvania: Christian Publications, 1982).
12. Virginia Postrel, *The Future and Its Enemies* (New York, 1998).

qualities that make men leaders of cultures (not just leaders of men). Finally, he must work relentlessly for the Christianization of culture.   Like Joseph, David, Deborah, and Daniel in the Bible, he must gain access to the instruments and institutions of cultural influence.   He must use them as a fulcrum by which to pervade every area of society with Christianity — not just personal salvation, but a full-orbed Christianity.

We must create *this* kind of Christian. Christian culture is won only by *this* kind of man or woman. Only *this* kind of Christian will lead the culture we must have. We must not remain comfortable with the *status quo*. Amid the present onslaught of a rapacious secularism and mounting Islam, business as usual will not suffice. We must create a dramatic reversal, adopt drastic measures, and employ a relentless strategy.

We will not drift into cultural leadership. It must be a conscious, unrelenting effort, one to which we must unreservedly commit our time, resources, and lives.

We sometimes eat in exquisite restaurants, and if the server brings us a dirty glass we do not say, "Well, that's O.K., because I'm sure the beverage you pour into the glass will be clean."   No, we know that the dirty glass will contaminate the beverage. We, likewise, are the receptacles of God's unvarnished Truth. Let us labor to be *clean* receptacles so that the cup of cold water that we offer a thirsty world is clean, pure, unadulterated.

CHAPTER 3

What is the Good News?

So here is the problem. Man is a guilty sinner,
God is a holy God. How can the two be brought together?
The answer is the cross of Christ.

Martyn Lloyd-Jones, *The Cross*[1]

"God was in Christ," writes Paul to the church at Corinth, "reconciling the world to Himself, not imputing [counting] their trespasses to [against] them (Second Epistle, 5:19).

Two thousand years ago, God acted dramatically in Jesus of Nazareth to bring back to Himself an estranged human race. This is the world's Good News — its best news, in fact — and in the Bible it is called the Gospel.[2] It was this message that formed the heart of the mission of Jesus' earliest followers after His death and resurrection. This *kerygma*, the Greek name for the apostolic proclamation, foreshadowed in the Old Testament, is revealed fully in the New Testament (see chapter 4). This, in fact, is likely the chief role of the New Testament in God's plan — to disclose the Good News to all of humanity. In theological language, the New Testament is principally the enumeration, interpretation and application of the redemptive events centered in the Person of Jesus Christ.[3] The Good News is that God hasn't left us to ourselves. The Good News is that God has *done something* by means of Jesus — actively taken the initiative — to bring us back into His good graces.

---

1. (Westchester, Illinois: Crossway, 1986), 33.
2. Alan Richardson, "Gospel," in ed., Richardson, *A Theological Word Book of the Bible* (New York: MacMillan, 1956), 100.
3. George E. Ladd, "The Knowledge of God: The Saving Acts of God," in ed., Carl F. H. Henry, *Basic Christian Doctrines* (New York: Holt Rinehart and Winston, 1962), 7-13.

What Is the Bad News?

The backdrop of the Good News is the bad news. In fact, we won't understand how good the *good* news really is until we grasp how dreadful the bad news really is.

The bad news is that humanity, and each of us as individuals, is sinful. What is sin? Sin is violating God's will for us as His rational creatures: breaking God's law — and His heart (1 Jn. 3:4). Our first parents, Adam and Eve, were created righteous. But they were also created with free will. They exercised that will to turn against the benevolent God Who had created them. Under the serpent's seduction, they wanted their way rather than God's way. They wanted self-autonomy. This is the heart of Original Sin — man's way rather than God's way.

We — all of us, all humans (except Jesus) — have followed our first parents in this sin. We're complicit in their sin (Rom. 5:12-21). We are liars and adulterers and hypocrites and rebels and racists and sexual deviants and cowards and bullies. We slander and covet and lust and profane God's holy name. We're envious and proud and resentful and thoughtless and uncharitable and faithless and domineering and self-serving (Rom. 3:10-23). Even our apparent virtues become vices in our proud, sinful hands. We're a bad lot, we sons of Adam, we daughters of Eve. Sin is a self-inflicted moral disease, and it plagues each of us.

This disease wreaks all the havoc we see in the world. It alienates us from one another. It alienates us from our environment, God's good creation. It even alienates us from ourselves — our greatest battles are those that enflame from our own bosom. Sin sets man not just against his fellow man and against his environment, but also against himself. Man is at war with himself because of his sin (Jas. 4:1-4).[4]

Worst of all, sin sets us against God. Sin alienates us from our Creator (Is. 59:2; Eph. 2:12). God is a righteous God, and we are *un*righteous people. God created us for fellowship with Him,

---

4. P. Andrew Sandlin, "Global Ecology and Godly Stewardship," *Free Inquiry*, April-May, 2008, 30-32.

but sin destroys that fellowship. This sin elicits a penalty — death (Rom. 5:12; 6:23a). God is righteous, and His righteousness demands that sin be dealt with righteously. Consequently, man in his natural state stands under a divine death sentence: eternal judgment by God (Jn. 3:18-20). If all men and women are sinners, and if God visits His judgment on all sinners, then the human race is condemned to God's judgment. This is the bad news.

The Good News is that the bad news is not the *last* news.

Good News for Sinners

God is not only a righteous God;. He's also a loving God (1 Jn. 4:8). When Adam and Eve sinned, God didn't throw them onto the cosmic ash heap. God created man (male and female), with His express purpose to enjoy us in an eternal relationship with Him; and He loves man as His good creation — a creation that has gone bad, but a good creation from His hand. In His love, God set in motion a great reclamation project. God's plan for humanity is to redeem, not destroy. God is not just man's awesome Judge; God is man's glorious Redeemer.

That redemption is found in Jesus Christ, the Son of God, very God of very God, in the words of the Nicene Creed. In His cruel death on the Cross, Jesus carried the punishment for the sins of the world (Jn. 1:29; Rom. 5:6-11; 1 Pet. 3:18). In His resurrection from the grave, He broke that very power of death that had shackled man from the Garden of Eden, and thereby showed God's acceptance of Christ's death as sufficient (1 Cor. 15:35-58). This redemptive work reconciled man to God (Eph. 2:11-13). Man is no longer alienated from God. Why? Because Jesus fulfilled the demand of God's justice — death, the penalty for sin (Rom. 3:24-25; 2 Cor. 5:21; 1 Pet. 2:24).[5]

God's love and His justice meet and look each other squarely in the eye at Calvary's cross. God loves sinful man, but His righteousness won't allow Him to excuse man's sin. The Cross is the

---

5. Leon Morris, *The Apostolic Preaching of the Cross* (Grand Rapids: Eerdmans, 1955, 1960).

great, public demonstration *both* of God's justice toward *and* His love for humanity. God imposed the righteous penalty for man's sin, and then God Himself — in His matchless love — paid the penalty in the Person of His Son, Jesus. God judged man, and then God Himself suffered His own judgment in Jesus Christ. Jesus died in the place of sinful man. And then Jesus rose triumphant over that sin, and ascended to sit with His Father in Heaven.

This is why Paul summarizes the Good News as the death, burial and resurrection of Jesus (1 Cor. 15:1-4).

Appropriating the Good News

The Good News carries a universal dimension. Jesus died for the sins of the world (1 Jn. 2:2). But all people are not saved. Salvation is not granted to all without qualification, *but only for those who trust in Jesus as their Savior and Lord.* Jesus' death and resurrection are sufficient for all but only effective for those who believe (Jn. 3:16-18).

Faith is the all-important factor here. God wanted to remove from salvation all self-autonomy (which got man into trouble in the first place). So, He arranged it that man could never get the credit. God alone gets the credit for man's salvation. Since salvation is not man's plan or by man's achievement, man can never boast (Eph. 2:8, 9). Man gets the benefit of Jesus' death and resurrection only if he *believes* — if he trusts in Jesus and Him alone for His salvation (Rom. 3:27-5:5; 10:9). Man is saved by *trusting* in Jesus Christ alone. Of course, this presupposes that man *understands* and *accepts* both the horror of his own sin and state, and the wonder of God's love, and therefore longs for that love and relationship. This faith, which is God's gift, rests on the promises of God — that if we trust in Jesus alone and all that He has done to redeem us, we will have eternal life. God requires that we rely on the work of Another, not on ourselves. Salvation is entirely by God's grace. *God actually saves us; He doesn't help us save ourselves.* Faith means resting on Jesus, not on ourselves.[6]

---

6   John Murray, *Redemption Accomplished and Applied* (Grand Rapids: Eerdmans, 1955), ch. 4.

But this faith is active, not passive — it hangs onto the good promises of God in Jesus and consecrates Christians to the Risen Christ.[7] It is not merely assent to religious beliefs, even the right beliefs; in addition, faith casts the sinner's life entirely on Jesus Christ. In appropriating His salvific work to us, faith alone saves, but the faith that saves is never alone. Faith without works is dead (Jas. 2:14-26). This faith that saves carries with it repentance, turning away from sin and turning toward God (Ac. 3:19; 2 Cor. 7:10). This faith that saves submits to Jesus as Lord and Master — it makes one a disciple (Mt. 16:24-27).[8] This faith submits, not only out of duty, but also out of amazement, and with a responsive love toward our merciful Lord.

The Good News puts man back into his proper place — as the glorified servant of God. And the Gospel exalts Jesus to His proper place — as the cosmic Lord and King of the living and the dead (Ac. 2:29-39; Rom. 14:9).

The faith that saves finds all its salvation, all its hope, all its peace, all its destiny in Jesus of Nazareth. In the lyrics of Robert Lowry's memorable hymn: "This is all my hope and peace, Nothing but the blood of Jesus/ This is all my righteousness, Nothing but the blood of Jesus." Salvation is entirely by God's grace, appropriated by an energetic, obedient faith in Jesus alone.

Conclusion

Ours tonight is a dignified dialogue about serious differences within Christendom. It is not a brush arbor camp meeting. But as a Gospel minister, I would be derelict in my duty if I neglected to say this: if you are here without Jesus Christ, you face God's awesome judgment. The Good News is that you need not face His judgment. Jesus died for your sins and for mine. If you place all your hope and trust in Jesus of Nazareth as your Savior and

---

7. Donald Bloesch, *Essentials of Evangelical Theology* (San Francisco: Harper & Row, 1978), 1:223-227.

8. James I. Packer, "Evangelicals and the Way of Salvation — New Challenges to the Gospel: Universalism, and Justification by Faith," in eds., Kenneth S. Kantzer and Carl F. H. Henry, *Evangelical Affirmations* (Grand Rapids: Zondervan, 1990), 130-131.

Lord, you can be saved tonight. If you turn from your sins and vest your faith in Jesus, you will become God's redeemed child this very evening.

If you understand and confess, your sins will be forgiven. God will wipe away all of your sins in the death and resurrection of Jesus, in Whom you trust. You will stand in Jesus' righteousness, justified in the sight of God. God will give you His Holy Spirit, Who will fill you and seal you until the day of your redemption. God will transform you from a rebel into an obedient son or daughter. You will be His disciple all the days of your life. You will become a member of the Lord's army, His church, called to exert stewardship of the earth for Christ the King, looking toward the day when all the nations bow in submission to King Jesus (Phil. 2:5-11). At Christ's Second Coming, you will be resurrected to bodily life on a renovated, resurrected earth; and you will live eternally on this renewed earth with all the saints and with God the Father, the Son and the Holy Spirit (Rev. 21:1-4). This eternal life is in Jesus Christ and in Him alone.

The Good News is that God has overcome the bad news in the death and resurrection of Jesus Christ.

CHAPTER 4

The *Kerygma* of the Kingdom

*The **basileia** is the great divine work of salvation in its fulfillment and consummation in Christ; the **ekklesia** is the
people elected and called by God and sharing in the bliss
of the **basileia**. Logically the **basileia** ranks first, and not
the **ekklesia**. The former, therefore, has a much more
comprehensive content.*

Herman Ridderbos, *The Coming of the Kingdom*[1]

What is the *Kerygma*?

Kerygma is an important word in Christianity. It is a Greek
word in the Bible that has been subsequently enlisted for its
great theological significance. It describes the earliest message of
the primitive Christian Faith ("preaching"). The *kerygma* is the ini-
tial apostolic preaching about Jesus Christ. It is the first message
that the apostles announced after Jesus rose from the dead and
ascended to heaven.[2]

The *kerygma* is so significant because it communicates what
the earliest followers of Jesus thought about Him and His ministry.
It is the news that they disseminated in the ancient Near East relat-
ing to the Person of Jesus Christ. What was this news? It is a cluster
of momentous, historical events that if one believes, his life will
change forever — notably that Jesus of Nazareth was the Son of
God, that He died for the human race on the Cross, that He rose
the third day from the dead in great victory, that He is returning
from Heaven in resplendent glory, and that whoever trusts in Him

---

1. (Philadelphia: Presbyterian and Reformed, 1962), 354, emphases in original.
2. U. Becker and D. Müller, "Proclamation, Preach, Kerygma," in ed., Colin Brown,
New International Dictionary of New Testament Theology (Grand Rapids: Zondervan, 1878,
1986), 3:44-48.

with a repentant, obedient faith will be granted eternal life by the grace of God.

This announcement centers on two main past[3] events — the death[4] and resurrection[5] of Jesus Christ. These events, according to the apostles, were necessary because of the massive plight of humanity that they are calculated to reverse — man's sin. Jesus died on the Cross as our sacrifice, paying the penalty for man's sin (1 Cor. 5:7; Eph. 5:2; 1 Pet. 3:18), and He rose from the dead to liberate us from the power of that sin (Rom. 6:1-13; 1 Pet. 3:21).

The heart of the *kerygma* is the death and resurrection of Jesus, the Cross and the empty tomb. This is the primitive apostolic message that we are called to perpetuate and preach today.

What is the Kingdom?

This *kerygma* must be set in the larger context of the Kingdom of God, the *basilea*, which literally denotes "rule" or "reign." It is not so much a realm over which a king reigns, as it is the reign itself.[6] We might say that the kingdom is wherever the king is.

Jesus centered His earthly ministry on the Kingdom of God. He states this fact quite explicitly from the very beginning (Mt. 4:17-23). This kingdom is the fulfillment of the Old Testament (Mt. 3:1-3). Jehovah had reigned over the earth since its creation, of course (Ps. 93, e.g.), and He was in a special sense the King of Israel (1 Sam. 8:1-9); but when Jesus arrived, He claimed to fulfill the prophesies of Messiah, Jehovah's unique representative in the earth and the King of the Jews. He embodied Jehovah's mediatory reign in the world. This is why Jesus asserts that His Father bestowed on Him a kingdom (Lk. 22:29). It is also why Paul writes that at the end of history, Jesus will restore His king-

---

3. The future event, the Second Advent, which is the culmination of the first two, is vital also, but is beyond the scope of this chapter.

4. P. T. Forsyth, *The Cruciality of the Cross* (Eugene, Oregon: Wipf and Stock, 1997).

5. Richard Gaffin, *Resurrection and Redemption* (Phillipsburg, New Jersey: Presbyterian and Reformed, 1978, 1987).

6. George E. Ladd, *Crucial Questions About the Kingdom of God* (Grand Rapids: Eerdmans, 1952), 77-81.

dom to the Father, to Whom the Son will then submit Himself (1 Cor. 15:23-28). The Kingdom of God in the interadvental age is the Kingdom of Jesus Christ. God grants His earthly rule to His Son Jesus. As we move progressively through the pages of the New Testament, we discover that this rule was not to be limited to the Jews. In Acts 2, for example, Peter declares in his Pentecostal sermon that the same Jesus Whom the Jews had crucified had been resurrected and had ascended to David's throne in Heaven. In other words, David's throne in Jerusalem had been transported to heaven, from which Jesus now reigns. When the Jews listening to Peter's sermon inquired what they should do, Peter responded that if they repented and trusted in Jesus and were baptized, they would be saved. The promise, He went on to say, was to them and their children, as well to those "afar off." This latter expression refers to believing Gentiles.

Even the Old Testament had predicted this universal reign. In Romans 15:12, Paul cites Isaiah that Jesus "will rise [from the dead] to reign over the Gentiles."

The *kerygma* is the heart of the Gospel, the Good News of salvation to all who believe (Rom. 3:22).

This relationship between the *kerygma* and the *basilea* implies that the Gospel is not an end in itself but subsists in order to extend the reign of God in the earth. The Kingdom is the reign of God in the earth by means of Jesus Christ, and the *kerygma* is the message that re-orients sinners so that they are restored to the proper relationship to the King.

Implications of the *Kerygma* of the Kingdom

Several implications relevant for the church today spring from this understanding of the *kerygma* and the Kingdom. I will state them in negative form and elaborate on each.

First, *soteriology is **not** the central theme of the Christian message.* Soteriology is that branch of theology that addresses salvation, especially the salvation of the individual. It is a crucial branch of theology, because the message of the Gospel is addressed first to individuals, and the Gospel of Jesus Christ is man's only hope of salvation. There will be no salvation apart from that Gospel. Soteriology summarizes the Biblical teaching regarding this individual salvation. As heirs of the Protestant Reformation, we hold to a distinctive soteriology — *solus Christus* (or *solo Christo*), *sola gratia*, and *sola fide* — we affirm that salvation is found only in Jesus Christ, not in the church; that this salvation is solely by the grace of God, not by man's meriting salvation in cooperation with God; and that justification is by faith alone, not by both faith and works (human merit or achievement before God).[7]

It was critical for the Reformation to stress these Biblical truths to counter certain errors that had crept into the Western church.

We heirs of this tradition must be careful, however, not to allow the leading concerns of the Reformation to shape the way we read the Bible.[8] The Bible, not our distinctives and confessions of faith, is preeminent (here we meet another Reformation "sola" — *sola Scriptura*, the Bible alone). And the Bible does not teach that individual soteriology is the overarching theme of the Faith or of the Bible. The great theme of the Bible is the glory of God manifested in Heaven and earth by means of God's kingdom. Soteriology is an indispensable segment of that Kingdom, but it does not exhaust that Kingdom. The Kingdom of God is much bigger than your salvation or mine, and God's plans for the world are larger than individual soteriology.[9]

Within the last 150 years or so in the West, both the *kerygma* and the Kingdom have been essentially reduced to "how to get to heaven when you die." This is not the message of Jesus or the early apostles.[10] Their message was the extension of God's earthly reign

---

7. Donald G. Bloesch, *Jesus Christ* (Downers Grove, Illinois: InterVarsity, 1997), 175-180.
8. Ned B. Stonehouse, "The Infallibility of Scripture and Evangelical Progress," in ed., Ronald Youngblood, *Evangelicals and Inerrancy* (Nashville: Nelson, 1984), 24.
9. This is where even the new "missional" churches can go astray in a truncated emphasis. See ed., Darrell L. Guder, *Missional Church* (Grand Rapids: Eerdmans, 1998). Just like individual soteriology, "mission" is not God's overarching plan for the church. That plan is to bring glory to God by the pervasiveness of Jesus' reign — the Kingdom.
10. John G. Stackhouse, "A Bigger — and Smaller — View of Mission," *Books & Culture*, May/June 2007, 26.

("the Kingdom"), to which the Gospel of Jesus makes an indispensable contribution. But if you heard many Western Christians only in the last few generations, you might get the idea that the Bible is chiefly about saving a few souls from the earth and getting them to Heaven when they die. If this is the main message of the Bible, God wasted a lot of ink, because the Bible addresses many more topics than soteriology, and it depicts some of those topics as no less significant than getting sinners to trust Jesus so they can get to Heaven. But since our era is increasingly man-centered, men want a God whose principal concern is their own salvation and not His own glory. He will not oblige them. The underlying theme of all that we read in the Bible is the glory of God as it comes to the fore in His Kingdom in human history. Doxology, not soteriology, comes first.

Second, *sinners **cannot** be saved unless they surrender to the Lordship (Kingship) of Jesus Christ.* We are saved by grace, but we are not saved without submission. This fact is clear from Jesus' statement that all those who do not take up their Cross and follow Him will lose their soul (that is, their life, Mt. 16:24-28). It is also evident from Jesus' promise to Zacchaeus, that God saved him when this tax collector pledged to restore all stolen property (Lk. 19:7-10). Moreover, Jesus told the wealthy young ruler that if he was not willing to surrender all that he has to follow Him, the man could not inherit eternal life (Lk. 18:18-23). If we do not bow the knee to King Jesus, we cannot be saved.

As a result, there can be no salvation without repentance. God does not merely save us in our sins; he saves us *from* our sins (Rom. 6-8).

Years ago in Mississippi I knew a preacher. He understood repentance. One day he was telling the Gospel to a young lady. She was a sinner who needed to get saved. For one thing, she was living with a young man and committing fornication. My friend told her that God would save her if she would repent and trust in Jesus. She said, "I can trust in Jesus, but I just can't give up sleeping with my boyfriend."

He replied to her, "Then you cannot get saved. God only

saves people who repent of their sins."

And my friend was right.

God will save all who come to him in faith, but we must come to Him on His terms, not our terms. Too many people act as though God is the great cosmic genie — existent to give them what they want, to make life better for them, to assist them in their self-improvement. They are in a tight jam with money or their job or their parents or children or the police or in their "relationships," and they need God to give them a quick fix, so they fly to Jesus with their problems. But Jesus saves *repentant* sinners, not sinners who want an existential quick fix.

To say we are saved totally by grace is not to say God requires nothing of us in salvation. You must lose your life in Jesus if you are to be saved — that is, you must die to yourself. Jesus says this plainly, so there's no use denying it. *If you are not ready to give up your life, you are not ready to get saved.*

Recently I was re-reading in Dietrich Bonhoeffer's classic *The Cost of Discipleship.* Bonhoeffer was a German Lutheran pastor in the '30s. He was a brilliant young theologian. Karl Barth called his first doctoral dissertation (which he completed when he was 24 years old) a "theological miracle." Bonhoeffer was implicated in several attempts to assassinate Hitler (Bonhoeffer, you see, was not one of those preachers who believed that Faith only applied in the church; he knew that if Jesus is Lord, He is Lord of all the earth.) He was executed in April 1945 for his complicity against Hitler, just three weeks before the city was liberated by the Allies.

In his book he talks about "cheap grace." He means by this expression that grace was costly to Jesus, but that too many Christians think they can act any way they want, since salvation is by God's grace. Grace is cheap — "free for all." We do not value it since it did not cost us anything. We tend to value something that costs us a lot, but we tend not to value something that does not cost us dearly. Jesus' death did not cost us anything, so we can easily cheapen that grace by which we receive the benefits of that death.

But this idea is a destructive evil. Bonhoeffer wrote, "The word of cheap grace has been the ruin of more Christians than any commandment of works."[11] And he is right.

I once heard Professor John Franke of Biblical Seminary relate something that a new Christian friend had told him. "Being a Christian costs you *nothing* since Jesus did all the work of salvation for you. But being a Christian costs you *everything*, since when you come to Jesus, you lose your life for Him." This is just what Jesus said in John 12:25-26. If you refuse to lose your life for Jesus — if you insist on doing things your way and not God's way — you cannot be saved. Grace if free, but it is not cheap.

Jesus died, and we follow Him in death — not a martyr's death (though we may have to do that, too), but death to ourselves. That's what it means to be saved, to be a follower of Jesus.

There is no salvation without surrender to the Kingship of Jesus Christ.

Third, *the church is **not** God's chief concern in the earth.* The fact that this assertion would be controversial shows how far the church has drifted from the Bible.[12] Jesus spoke again and again about the kingdom, but only twice about the church (by which he could simply have meant His followers in a generic sense, and not an institution[13]). By the church, the Bible denotes the *ekklesia*, the people of God in a particular locale under the oversight of leaders (1 Pet. 5:1-5).[14] The Bible teaches that Jesus shed His blood for this church (Ac. 20:28) and that He rules in this church (Eph. 1:18-23). It is tempting to presume that the church is a sort of idealized body known only to God, but this is not how the Bible uses the term. When we say the church, we denote God's people in a specific location, not an "invisible" church; not a human institution as such; and not (worse yet) a denomination, of which the Bible knows nothing. Rather, the denotation of *ekklesia* in the Bible is: God's collective, localized body covenanted together and with Jesus under His authority.

---

11. Dietrich Bonhoeffer, *The Cost of Discipleship* (New York: MacMillan, 1937, 1959), 59.

12. Wolfhart Pannenberg, *Theology and the Kingdom of God* (Philadelphia: Westminster, 1969), 76-77.

13. Donald E. Gowan, "Church," in ed., Gowan, *The Westminster Theological Wordbook of the Bible* (Louisville and London: Westminster John Knox Press, 2003), 63.

14. L. Coenen, "Church, Synagogue," in ed., Colin Brown, *The New International Dictionary of New Testament Theology*, 1:291-292.

Tragically, in Christian history the church has often been identified with the Kingdom of God. This is the position of the Roman Catholic Church.[15] It is also the view of the Westminster Confession of Faith (ch. 25, no. 2). But it is not the view of the Bible. It is almost self-evident from the pages of the New Testament that the kingdom is the reign of God and that the church is an *aspect* of that reign (e.g., 1 Cor. 15:24, 50).

This means that Christian schools and businesses and politics and music and pro-life and family and campus and cultural and mercy ministries and so on are (or should be) within the Kingdom of God, even though they are not specifically the church — that is, they are not the specific community assembling under Jesus' Lordship (though the individuals engaging in these activities are often part of the church). The church is the assembly of the faithful, and they act as the church when they act faithfully wherever they are; but the Kingdom is the sphere of Jesus Christ's rule, and the church is only one crucial aspect of it.[16]

The Kingdom, not the church, is the big issue. "The mission of the church is to herald the coming kingdom of God, but the church must never mistake itself for the kingdom . . . ."[17]

Fourth, **no** *man or human institution may arrogate to itself the claims of Jesus as rightful King.* Man likes to play God. This was the Original Sin of Eve in the Garden of Eden (Gen. 3:1-6). In Babel man tried to erect a tower rising up to God (Gen. 11:1-9). Because man is a sinner, he cannot accept that God is God and that he is not God. God rules man by His love and justice, but man wishes to control and tyrannize his fellow man.

This happens in the family. Oriental cultures tend to worship ancestors; this is pagan practice. In contemporary Christian circles, we have the "patriarchy" movement, which rightly stresses the father's leadership in the family, but too often it makes the

---

15. *Catechism of the Catholic Church* (Washington, D.C.: United States Catholic Conference [Libreria Editrice Vaticana], 1994, 2nd edition), 138-143.
16. Donald E. Gowan, "Kingdom of God, Kingdom of Heaven," in ed., Gowan, *The Westminster Theological Wordbook of the Bible*, 274-278.
17. Donald G. Bloesch, *Jesus Christ*, 243.

Christian father the final earthly arbiter of family life. It is legalistic. Its proponents sometimes claim that birth control is sin, that Sunday school is sin, that sending daughters off to college is sin, and that the husband is "responsible" for his wife's sins (this is the "Federal Headship" theory). In some quarters, women are to be seen and not heard. The husband becomes "God's representative" (too often the tyrant) in the home.

Today, also, there is a prominent tendency to the return to "high-church" public worship patterns. It is held that God is our Father but the church is our mother, a travesty of church tradition that the Bible nowhere teaches. It is asserted or implied that salvation is dispensed at the hands of priests or elders in baptism or the Eucharist. Even some Protestants declare that union with the local church (in water baptism) effects a sort of saving union with Jesus Christ.[18] All of these ecclesial views compromise the Creator-creature distinction and invite an impoverishment of the Gospel. The church is not the extension of the incarnation of Jesus, and any ecclesiology (view of the church) that subordinates soteriology to the church is on an idolatrous track.

While family and the church are legitimate, divinely established institutions, beware of any theology that confounds divine authority with human authority, that situates the dispensing of eternal salvation in the hands of man, or that tries to monopolize the work of God in the earth.

Fifth, and finally, *God's objective is **not** merely to save elect sinners but to redeem all of life and society and culture — the entire world.* Paul writes that Jesus will rule in the present age until He subordinates all enemies except death itself (1 Cor. 15:20-28). The writer of Hebrews states that all things have been placed under the Lord's authority (Heb. 2:5-9). The sweep of redemption is as comprehensive as the sweep of sin.[19] God is redeeming all that is sinful

---

18. Douglas Wilson, "Union with Christ: An Overview of the Federal Vision," in ed., E. Calvin Beisner, *The Auburn Avenue Theology: Pros and Cons* (Fort Lauderdale, Florida: Knox Theological Seminary, 2004), 5-6.

19. Cornelius Van Til, *An Introduction to Systematic Theology* (Phillipsburg, New Jersey: Presbyterian and Reformed, 1974, 1982), 133.

(Rom. 8:20-25). The Second Adam is winning back all that the first Adam lost in Eden (Rom. 5:12-21).

The Gospel is a regal Gospel, and the goal of the Gospel is to bring the world under the authority of Jesus Christ (Phil. 2:4-11).

For too long the church has bought into a dualism — a sacred-secular distinction that sees church and home life and Bible reading and evangelism (narrowly considered) as "spiritual," but education and technology and science and politics and economics as "worldly." This dualism has surrendered vast cultural territories to unbelievers and to secularists. Ironically, many Christians complain about the condition of the culture, yet it has been their own dualistic dereliction that has permitted this de-Christianization (secularization) of society.

God is interested not just in the family and church, but in the entire world.

As heirs of the King (Rom. 8:17), we are commanded to call the entire world to be reconciled to God in the Person and work of Jesus Christ (2 Cor. 5:19). The Great Commission requires that we preach the Gospel, baptize and disciple all the nations for Jesus, to whom all authority in heaven and on earth has been given (Mt. 28:18-20). "When we preach Christ," writes Pinnock, "we are not just offering a happiness pill and hell-fire insurance, we are asking people to join in the dominion mandate and come aboard the kingdom train."[20]

This means that, among other things, we should encourage our young people to enter not just the full-time Christian ministry (pastors and missionaries and teachers, who are sorely needed), but also fields such as sales and medicine and technology and music and politics and business professions. There are no "secular" occupations as long as they are surrendered to Jesus Christ.

If God's objective is to bring the entire world under the authority of King Jesus, then our commission must be to extend that kingdom far beyond the four walls of the church. The *kerygma* is

---

20. Clark H. Pinnock, *Three Keys to Spiritual Renewal* (Minneapolis: Bethany House, 1985), 78.

the Gospel message at the center of the *basileia* (kingdom), defined as the reign of God in the earth; **but the Kingdom of God is God's great work in the earth.**

CHAPTER 5

Biblical Salvation Changes Lives

Know ye not that the unrighteous shall not inherit
the kingdom of God? Be not deceived: neither fornicators,
nor idolaters, nor adulterers, nor effeminate, nor abusers
of themselves with mankind, Nor thieves, nor covetous,
nor drunkards, nor revilers, nor extortioners,
shall inherit the kingdom of God.

1 Corinthians 6:9-10

Therefore if any man [be] in Christ,
[he is] a new creature: old things are passed away;
behold, all things are become new.

2 Corinthians 5:17

This message is an excursus from or a sidebar about 1
Corinthians. It flows from Paul's comments and it should
flood our heart. The message will start with a theology lesson and
end with an exhortation. It will be simple, concrete, and direct.

It is clear from vv. 9-10 (1 Cor. 6) that we can't expect to
see the kingdom in the end if we live lives dominated by sin.[1] It's
not the only text in the Bible to say or imply this warning. Jesus
said that we'll stand under God's judgment if we don't forgive our
brother from our heart (Mt. 18:35). In fact, Jesus also said that
if we don't forgive our brother, God won't forgive us (Mt. 6:15).
John tells us that the person who makes a practice of sinning, that
is, who keeps on sinning without righteousness, is "of the devil" (1
Jn. 3:4-9). We can't cut these teachings out of the Bible; we can't
pretend as though they don't exist. The Bible teaches that *if you*

---

1. I am generally sympathetic with the exegesis of these verses by Gordon Fee, *The First Epistle to the Corinthians* (Grand Rapids: Eerdmans, 1987), 242-248.

act a certain way in this life, you cannot expect to be saved in the end. It's as simple and profound as that.

How does this teaching coincide with the teaching that salvation is entirely by God's grace, apart from good works (Eph. 2:8-9)? First, know this: Our minds are finite. One of our big problems in interpreting the Bible is trying to reconcile seemingly contradictory texts. Sometimes we can't. That was the view of Cornelius Van Til, and I agree with him.[2] Think of the Trinity. We know that God is both One and Three — one Person and three Persons. He is one Person in the same sense that He is three Persons. God isn't less personal than Jesus, for example. So, how do we explain this? It seems like a logical contradiction. It is a logical contradiction, but it is what the Bible teaches, and I believe it.

God is sovereign over all things. He knows the end from the beginning because He makes all things come to pass. Yet He's not the author of sin. How can this be? How can we reconcile these two views logically? We can't. We believe the Bible even when we can't logically reconcile all of its teachings.

The same is true in the case of God's grace and man's obligation. The Bible teaches that salvation is totally of grace, God's work from beginning to end, without man's work or merit or achievement. But it also teaches that man has obligations in salvation. How do we reconcile these two facts? We don't. We just believe and teach both of them. Let's explore the relationship between the two.

Lordship Salvation

About 20 years ago a controversy erupted in evangelicalism (imagine that!). It came to be called the "Lordship Salvation" controversy. On one side were the folks who *opposed* what they labeled "Lordship Salvation."[3] These included men like Charles Ryrie

---

2. Cornelius Van Til, *The Defense of the Faith* (Phillipsburg, New Jersey: Presbyterian and Reformed, 1955 edition), 44, 45, 160.
3. Charles Ryrie, *Balancing the Christian Life* (Chicago: Moody, 1969), ch. 17 and Zane Hodges, *Absolutely Free!* (Grand Rapids: Zondervan, 1989).

and Zane Hodges. Here was their view (in summary). God saves you totally by grace through faith in Jesus. When you trust Jesus, you trust Him as your Savior. Salvation is entirely by grace apart from man's works. When you trust Jesus, therefore, you trust Him *only* as your Savior. You don't trust Him as your Lord and Master. Mainly this means that when you trust Jesus, you don't make a commitment to be His disciple. Commitment to Jesus as Lord is good and desirable, but that comes later in the Christian life. In other words, salvation is to be separated from discipleship. Jesus wants disciples, but you can be a Christian without being a disciple. So, we'd sometimes hear preachers saying, "Years ago some of you here trusted Jesus as your Savior, but now you need to trust Him as your *Lord*. You're saved, you're Christians, but you're not disciples." Their leading point was that if you add commitment to salvation, you're denying salvation by grace.

Then there was the opposing view. This is the side that *did* believe in "Lordship Salvation." It was led by folks like John McArthur and John Gerstner.[4] Their position is basically this. They agreed that God saves sinners totally by grace through faith in Jesus. They agreed that salvation is by grace through faith alone apart from works. But they did not agree that you can trust Jesus as Savior without trusting Him as Lord. For one thing, you can't trust a divided Christ. (That's how A. W. Tozer put it.[5]) Jesus is both Savior and Lord, and you can't divide up His offices when you receive Him. That would be like saying, "I take this woman to be my wife, but I do not take her to be the mother of my children." No woman — at least no sensible woman — would tolerate that doublespeak. Wifehood and motherhood reside in one woman. To take a woman as a wife is to take her as the mother of your children. You can't have one without the other.

Similarly, you can't take Jesus as your Savior without taking

---

4. John McArthur, *The Gospel According to Jesus* (Grand Rapids: Zondervan, 1988) and John Gerstner, *Wrongly Dividing the Word of Truth* (Brentwood, Tennessee: Wolgemuth & Hyatt, 1991), ch. 13.
5. A. W. Tozer, "No Saviorhood Without Lordship," *The Root of the Righteous* (Harrisburg, Pennsylvania: Christian Publications, 1955), 83-86.

Him as your Lord. The Jesus Who saves you is the Jesus Who rules you — and the Rulership is no less optional than the Saviorhood. No sincere Christian would say, "I can have eternal life without Jesus as my Savior." You know that salvation resides in Jesus alone. But we must with equal force deny this statement: "I can have eternal life without Jesus as my Lord." No Saviorhood without Lordship.

The second big problem with the non-Lordship idea is that it tends to make Jesus into a celestial genie — His chief job is to give us what we desire; His role is to occupy the center of our self-help and self-image programs. "Jesus helps me realize my potential" — the Christianized version of today's ubiquitous "Human Potential Movement." That is a popular idea these days, and it's nearly blasphemous. Many people see the Gospel as the Spiritual Gravy Train — "It meets all my desires down here and in the end deposits me squarely at Heaven's pearly gates."

What do we say to this? Let's look at the words of Jesus (Mt. 16:24-26):

> Then Jesus said to His disciples, "If anyone desires
> to come after Me, let him deny himself, and take up
> his cross, and follow Me. For whoever desires to save
> his life will lose it, but whoever loses his life for My
> sake will find it. For what profit is it to a man if he
> gains the whole world, and loses his own soul? ..."

I draw your attention to the fact that if you don't lose your life in following Jesus, you'll lose your soul. This according to Jesus. Salvation necessitates discipleship, and if you refuse to be a disciple, you can kiss eternal life goodbye.

In the simple words of Daniel P. Fuller, *only disciples are saved.*[6]

If you're here today, and you're not a disciple of Jesus, you're not a Christian; you have no eternal life; you are headed for Hell.

---

6. Daniel P. Fuller, "Only Disciples Are Saved," http://www.fuller.edu/ministry/berean/disciple.htm [accessed June 28, 2008].

I don't care how young or old you are. I don't care if you said yes to Jesus a million times, if you're not a disciple, you're not saved.

The idea that somebody can be a Christian without being a disciple is false doctrine. It sends people to Hell, and it must be challenged.

Nominal Churchianity

Today we have another grave problem: "Nominal Churchianity." It goes like this. If you have made a profession of faith and are baptized and join the church, you're a Christian, or at least considered one, enjoying benefits of saving union with Christ.[7] Now, there's an element of truth here, and we dare not miss it. If someone comes here and professes faith in Jesus and is baptized in water and joins the church, we don't begin by *doubting* he's a Christian. We take him at his profession (same with baptized infants; we treat them as the Lord's lambs, not little pagans[8]). We give professors the benefit of the doubt. They profess publicly and formally at baptism. Baptism is important. It's a mark of identification. It identifies you with the crucified and risen Lord (Rom. 6:1-4). It links you with a particular history — redemptive history.[9] It enrolls you in the visible people of God, the church. But it doesn't make any internal change in anybody. It's much like circumcision was in the old covenant. It enrolled you as part of the visible people of God (the local church, both Old and New Testaments), but it didn't save anybody. God told Israel, "You may have been circumcised in your flesh, but you need to get circumcised in your heart" (Dt. 10:16; 30:6). You could be a part of Israel in the flesh and yet not truly a part of Israel (Rom. 2:28-29). You could be of the physical seed of Abraham and yet not be

---

7. Peter J. Leithart, "Trinitarian Anthropology: Toward a Trinitarian Re-casting of Reformed Theology," in ed., E. Calvin Beisner, *The Auburn Avenue Theology: Pros and Cons* (Fort Lauderdale, Florida: Knox Theological Seminary, 2004), 68-71.
8. Robert S. Rayburn, "The Presbyterian Doctrines of Covenant Children, Covenant Nurture, and Covenant Succession," *Presbyterion* 22/2 (1996), 76-112.
9. G. C. Berkouwer, *The Sacraments* (Grand Rapids: Eerdmans, 1969), 117.

Abraham's true children (Jn. 8:31-47).[10]

Baptism in water (like Old Testament circumcision) places you into the visible covenant body; it doesn't place you into the new covenant.[11] In the new covenant, God gives you a new heart by the blood-shedding of Jesus (Heb. 8). You can be enrolled in the visible people of God without being a part of Jesus. There are so many examples of this in the Bible that for somebody to deny it, he needs his head examined. In fact, in Israel's history, sometimes, the vast majority of people were not even followers of Jehovah (Rom. 9:24-29). They were part of the people of God but lacked eternal life.

The same is true in the New Testament era. That's why Paul writes that if we depart from the Gospel, we have believed in vain (1 Cor. 15:2), and why Peter warns us to make our calling and election certain (2 Pet. 1:10).

The idea that everybody who's baptized and a church member is saved, a Christian, a part of the vine, a sheep, headed for the Kingdom of God isn't just silly. It's dangerous. It provides false relief for hypocrites. It says that salvation is in the hands of the church. "God is your Father and the church is your mother." What a load of rubbish. Friends, Hell will be populated by plenty of baptized, professed Christians.

Now, all sorts of people claim to be Christian but live lives of rabid disobedience. The cruelest thing we could do is to give them the comfort that they're Christians. Christians are disciples; and if you're not a disciple, you're not a Christian.

Jesus said that at the Final Judgment. "Depart from me, I never knew you":

Paul said nothing about baptism in 1 and 2 Thessalonians. According to 1 Cor. 1:13-17 he preferred not to baptize,

---

10. For a remarkably balanced perspective on the efficacy of water baptism, see Richard L. Pratt, Jr., "Baptism as a Sacrament of the Covenant," in ed., John H. Armstrong, *Understanding Four Views of Baptism* (Grand Rapids: Zondervan, 2007), 59-72.
11. In contradistinction to Steve Wilkins, "Covenant, Baptism, and Salvation," in ed., Steve Wilkins and Duane Garner, *The Federal Vision* (Monroe, Louisiana: Athanasius Press, 2004), 54-61.

because he feared that those he baptized would feel superior to those baptized by less prominent church leaders. This reluctance (v. 15) implies that the public, official nature of baptism — vital for marking Christians off from the godless society around them — nevertheless carries with it the danger that baptized people, like the Jews with their circumcision, would think that the rite, by itself, enhances one's acceptance with God. On the other hand, a refusal to be baptized is unacceptable, because an unwillingness to stand up and be counted as Jesus' disciple implies a lack of confidence in what he will do for one's future.[12]

All Christians persevere; if they don't, they were never Christians.

Salvation from Sin

Can you get saved without giving up your sin? No! God saves us *from* something. He saves us not just from Hell. He saves us from our sin. Jesus on the Cross saved us from the penalty of sin. When God justified us He saved us from the power of sin. When the Spirit regenerated us He saved us from the pleasure of sin. One day when we see the Lord He'll save us from the very presence of sin.

No person is sinlessly perfect. If we say that we have not sinned, we deceive ourselves and the truth is not in us. John the apostle tells us this (1 Jn. 1:8). This is why we need to plead the blood and forgiveness of Jesus every day — not just on Sunday (v. 9).

But salvation *does* save us from something, and that something is sin. You can't have Jesus and your sin too.

Let's take a plump pig. We get the pig from a pig farmer. We take the pig home and give the pig a bath. We primp the pig. We spray perfume onto its big snout. We powder the pig's face and back. We tie an ornate, gold ribbon around the pig's fatty neck. And we situate the pig on our gorgeous leather sofa for all visitors to see. When the door is open, and the pig gets one good chance,

---

12. Fuller, "Only Disciples Are Saved."

what will he do? He'll head for the mud hole or the refuse outside. Why? *Because it's in the nature of a pig to love mud.* Why doesn't he love to stay inside? Because it's not in the nature of the pig to sit indoors on leather sofas with a perfumed snout. Pigs love slop.

On the other hand, we take a little clean lamb. We take it from its mother in the flock and put it in a slimy swine's mud hole. What will it do? It will leap out and shake itself and try to get clean. Why? *It's not in the nature of a lamb to like mud.*

Listen well. Sometimes pigs find their way into ornate mansions, but it's not in their nature to stay there. Sometimes lambs find their way into hog pens, but it's not in their nature to stay there.

Likewise, sometimes unbelievers profess faith in Jesus, get baptized, join the church, clean up on the outside, quit all of their vices — for a while. But in time, the strain and pressure are all too hard. They're overcome by their nature; they head for the world's pigpen. On the other hand, Christians often commit sin — horrendous sin like adultery and homosexuality and murder — but Christians repent and turn back to God. Why? Because it's not in their nature to revel in sin.

Some of you have been chasing relatives that head for the depraved mud hole every good chance they get. And you get tired of chasing. They once made a profession of faith and got baptized and joined the church, and you say, "They should be acting like Christians!" Likely the reason they aren't acting like it, is that they're not . . . Christians. We should be realistic and quit expecting them to act like Christians when in fact, they're not.

Paul says that if any person is in Christ, he's a new creation. Children, this applies to you, too. If you care nothing for the things of God; if you delight in sin and despise righteousness; if your parents are always dragging you kicking and screaming and oinking out of the slop, you have every reason to believe that you're a hog, not a lamb. Lambs fall into mud holes, but they don't revel in mud holes. They don't like to stay there. If you love to revel in depravity, that's because you're not a child of God but a child of the Devil.

Jesus is both Savior and Lord. When you come to Jesus, you do not come with conditions. He sets the conditions, and you submit to the conditions if you want to have eternal life.

What a glorious truth! Today if you're without Jesus, you're without hope, lost in your sins and headed for damnation. BUT . . . God loves you. He has made a way of salvation in His Son Jesus. Jesus died on the Cross in your place and mine. He rose the third day from the grave and defeated sin and the world and the Devil. If you'll place your hope in Him today, if you'll say, "I trust in You and not myself; I turn my life over to You. I am not my own. I now belong to You," you will be gloriously saved.

You need a new Savior, and you need a new Lord.

Jesus is both.

CHAPTER 6

Transformation by Resurrection

What shall we say then? Shall we continue in sin that grace may abound? Certainly not! How shall we who died to sin live any longer in it? Or do you not know that as many of us as were baptized into Christ Jesus were baptized into His death? Therefore we were buried with Him through baptism into death, that just as Christ was raised from the dead by the glory of the Father, even so we also should walk in newness of life. For if we have been united together in the likeness of His death, certainly we also shall be in the likeness of His resurrection, knowing this, that our old man was crucified with Him, that the body of sin might be done away with, that we should no longer be slaves of sin. For he who has died has been freed from sin. Now if we died with Christ, we believe that we shall also live with Him, knowing that Christ, having been raised from the dead, dies no more. Death no longer has dominion over Him. For the death that He died, He died to sin once for all; but the life that He lives, He lives to God.

Romans 6:1-10

Paul has just been teaching that Jesus is running up the score on the Devil. Where sin abounded, grace abounded much more (Rom. 5:20). In other words, where there's lots of sin, God not just forgives that sin (if we repent, of course) but showers His grace and obliterates that sin.

But people might get the idea that, since lots of our sin elicits a shower of grace, why not sin more and more so that God can shower His grace more and more? "This grace is so great, let's just keep sinning so we can get more grace." Then, sin might end up being a good thing after all, since it highlights God's grace.

Paul's answer (v. 1) is, well ... no. God's grace overwhelms our sin, but please understand one important thing: God's grace isn't designed just to forgive sin; *God's grace is designed ultimately to get rid of sin.* Paul's whole point early in Romans is how God gets rid of man's sin. God's not just trying to forgive sin; His objective is to *destroy* sin. Sin destroys man, and God — by His grace — destroys sin. The goal of grace is to destroy sin, not just forgive it.[1] (This is why sanctification is no less important than justification, and you can never have one without the other.[2])

We read in Titus 2:11-12: "For the grace of God that brings salvation has appeared to all men, teaching us that, denying ungodliness and worldly lusts, we should live soberly, righteously, and godly in the present age . . . ."

So, if there's anybody that says, "Well, I know sin is bad, but I can keep sinning since God's grace will always forgive me," he or she is on the road to destruction. That's not grace; that's a *dis*grace. "Shall we sin that grace may abound? May it never be!"

And in saying no, Paul brings up one of the most remarkable truths in all the Bible. It's this: that when Jesus died on the Cross and rose from the grave, in some sense we died and rose with Him. Remarkable. What does this mean? Paul is saying that what died when Jesus died was the power of sin over Jesus, and what came alive when Jesus rose was the great new power of righteousness (vv. 6 and 10). And we died to sin and we rose in righteousness right along with Him.

It's hard to tell you how momentous this teaching is. We'll get back to it in a minute.

But first, Paul brings up baptism. He's not trying to give some sort of "baptismal theology." He's trying to make a bigger point, and baptism helps him make it.

When you're baptized, you're baptized *into* something. For instance, you remember John the Baptist, Jesus' cousin, who baptized Jesus? Well, when you are baptized into someone's name, you really say that you're becoming that person's disciple (Ac. 19:3).

---

1. Norman Shepherd, *The Call of Grace* (Phillipsburg, New Jersey: P & R Publishing, 2000), 104.
2. Alister McGrath, *Justification by Faith* (Grand Rapids: Zondervan, 1988), ch. 2.

The men who were baptized in the name of John were baptized to become John's disciples or followers. When you are baptized in the name of Jesus, you publicly say you become *His* followers. Baptism is a public attestation of discipleship.

But Christian baptism in water signifies something deeper. It signifies union with Jesus Himself. You see, when we trust Jesus, we are united to Him. But becoming a part of Him means to share in His death and resurrection.

The big issue is not the baptism in water. It's like circumcision in the Old Testament. Baptism is supposed to signify something else, a deeper reality. Baptism in water (as we saw in the preceding chapter) signifies our union with Jesus Christ and His death and resurrection.

This is why the Baptists believe in baptism by immersion: you are immersed, laid out and then brought up out of the water. I'm not persuaded by their view, but it does make a good point: baptism signs our union with Jesus in His death and resurrection. This is where Paul gets really interesting.

Now, remember from Romans chapters 1-3 that the big deal for Paul is how God is going to overcome all this sin that has infested the world. Because of Adam and Eve's sin, the world has turned into this big, poison-infested swamp. We're in it, and this fetid swamp-water gushes over us and dirties us, and it influences all we do. In fact, the swamp water comes from our own insides — our own sin pollutes the worldly swamp we're swimming in.

How God Gets Rid of Sin

The big question for Paul is *how God gets rid of the poison in the swamp*. That answer has two parts. First, recall that God justifies us in the blood of Jesus. Jesus took our place on the Cross. He bore our penalty. We no longer will face punishment for our sin since Jesus was punished in our place. God has justified us by faith — we trust in Jesus. "Justification by faith alone"[3] (Rom. 4:5). So now our guilt before God is wiped away in the blood of Jesus. The

---

3. G. C. Berkouwer, *Faith and Justification* (Grand Rapids: Eerdmans, 1954), ch. 7.

penalty of sin is done away with in God's court.[4]

But man's problem isn't just the guilt of sin. Man's problem is the pollution and corruption of sin. Sin pollutes the swamp. How does God clean up the swamp?

By the resurrection of Jesus. That's what the next few chapters of Romans are all about. It's not enough to be justified by the death of Jesus. We have to be cleaned up by the *life* of Jesus.

So, what's the big deal about this? It's this: Jesus' resurrection changed Him. And in getting to this, we're getting to Paul's major point. *Jesus himself was transformed when He rose from the dead* (as Richard Gaffin has so insightfully noted[5]). When Jesus died, He died in weakness; but He was raised in power (1 Cor. 15:42-45).

In other words, Jesus' earthly existence was not His resurrection existence. Today, Jesus is not the same as He was when He walked on the earth and died on the Cross. It's the same Jesus, *but He is a changed Man.*

And because Jesus is a changed man, since we are united to Him in His resurrection, we are changed men and women. That is how God changes us. **God changes us by having changed Jesus.**

Think hard about this. When Jesus died, He was bound by sin. Sin had power over Him — not His sin, of course, but ours. Notice v. 9. Before Jesus rose, sin and death had power over Him. Jesus was enslaved to the power of sin — not His own sin, of course, but ours. He carried our sin, our grief and sorrows (Is. 53). His life was one of weakness and illness and weariness and tragedy and loneliness — the life of sin-bearing. Sin, our sin, which He carried during His earthly life, had power over Him.

This is the earthly Jesus, the Son of God, Whom we read about in the Gospels. This is the life of Jesus all the way to the Cross and to the tomb in which He was buried. If you want to know the "life of Christ" according to Paul, it was a life of weakness, grief, burdens, illness, hardship — on the Cross, it was even a

---

4. Leon Morris, *The Atonement* (Leicester, England: InterVarsity, 1983), ch. 8

5. Richard Gaffin, *Resurrection and Redemption* (Phillipsburg, New Jersey: Presbyterian and Reformed, 1978, 1987), 78-92.

life separated from the Father, Who abandoned His own Son, the Son Who carried our sins.

This is the earthly life of Jesus Christ that we read about in the Bible.

The momentous teaching of Romans 6, 1 Cor. 15 and 2 Cor. 5 is that in that empty tomb 2000 years ago, *Jesus left that life behind.* Jesus was transformed.

Let me explain further. Just as the Son of God entered a new mode of existence — a new way of living — when He was conceived in Mary's womb, so He entered a new mode of existence — a new way of living — when He rose from the dead. When Jesus came to earth to be born, He laid aside His way of life with the Father (Phil. 2:5-8). He gave up the glories of Heaven for a life of suffering and humiliation — for us. When He was conceived in the womb and born in Bethlehem, He abandoned His previous way of life for a life of sin-bearing and weakness and loneliness and defeat. He assumed a new, humble mode of existence.

But now we must understand that when Jesus rose from the grave, He abandoned that humble, earthly way of life for a new life. He was sown in weakness; He was raised in power. He gave up His life of sin-bearing and weakness and loneliness and defeat for a life of power and joy and communion and victory. The old Man Jesus became the new Man Jesus. Jesus had an old man and a new man (Paul's language) just like we do. And the old Man Jesus is gone forever.

Paul makes much the same point in 2 Cor. 5:16-17, where He's talking about the resurrection. He says that even if we once knew Christ according to the flesh, that is, in a natural way, yet now we don't know him that way any longer. We cannot know Christ as we once knew him. He has changed, and we have changed.

If you want to know the Jesus that now exists, read the book of Revelation, not the Gospels. In Revelation, He is the conquering King, progressively beating down the old dragon (Satan); punishing His enemies on earth who are at war with Him; and delivering His people, who love and obey Him. He is not just the Lamb Who was slain but the Lion Who flexes his authority over the earth. He is the Jesus at whose holy, horrifying presence John fell down as one dead.

This Jesus — not the Jesus of the Gospels — is the Jesus alive today.

Jesus' New Life and Ours

This fact has staggering implications for Paul. It means that since Jesus has a new mode of existence, a new life, *we do also.* We are united to Him, so when He died to sin, we died to it also. When He rose to righteousness, we rose also. Why is it necessary to be united with Jesus? Because that is God's way of destroying sin! Read v. 6 carefully.

Understand, therefore: we can longer encounter — no longer have a personal relationship with — the crucified Lord. We can only encounter and relate to and love and befriend the crucified Lord *in His resurrected state.* Think of it. What kind of existence does Jesus have today? Can He die (v. 9)? Can His life today be filled with sin-bearing, sorrow, loneliness and weakness? No, it cannot. Well, then *neither must ours.* That's Paul's whole point in this section.

Jesus calls us to take up our cross daily and follow Him (Lk. 9:23). Paul says that he dies daily (1 Cor. 15:31). And in passages like Mt. 10:38, 2 Cor. 1:5-7, 4:10, Phil. 3:10, and Col. 1:24, we are informed that our present life must include suffering, just as our Lord's earthly life did. But for the Christian, *there can be no death without a resurrection, just as for Christ there could not be.* Every death entails a resurrection, including our future physical death and future resurrection. But in the present life, you cannot die every day to sin and self without also being resurrected to righteousness and power and hope and joy and glory and victory.

Christians do not live the crucified life; they live the resurrection life.

What does this mean? It means that when we suffer, when we are lonely, when we are ill, when we are weak, we can appeal to Jesus, yes, but only to the Jesus Who lives today in constant *victory* over loneliness, suffering, illness, weakness. In other words, we cannot encounter a Jesus Who knows only loneliness, suffering, illness, weakness, *because that Jesus no longer exists.* We can only encounter a Jesus Who has defeated all of these. And if we are united to Him, we have also defeated them. We simply must live a life of resurrection — dead to sin, alive to Jesus (vv. 11-12). There is no other Christian life.

The wife of the best man in my wedding is a remarkable woman. I have known her for 40 years. Months after they were married, she and my best man were T-boned by a drunk driver. He was thrown clear, but her backbone was crushed. She was paralyzed and has been a paraplegic for over 30 years. I knew her when she was a teenager in full bloom and health. I cannot know Tina that way anymore. She is a new and different woman. Her life has been transformed.

In the same way, I cannot know the "old" Jesus that walked the earth. I can only know the "new" Jesus that rules in Heaven (1 Cor. 15:47-49).

To those of you who want to know Jesus in His pain and suffering and agony and weakness, who want Jesus to join you in wallowing in your self-doubt and failure and weakness, who desire for Him to be your partner in misery: You're too late; you missed Him; *you're 2000 years too late.* That Jesus has been transformed. He is now the Lord of cosmic glory, not the Jesus of the earthly humiliation.[6]

John on the island writes of this Jesus, quoting Him: "I [am] he that liveth, and was dead; and, behold, *I am alive for evermore*" (Rev. 1:17).

Conclusion

What does this mean for you and me? It means that when we come to Jesus for empathy and care and help (Heb. 4:14-16), we can come only to Jesus the Victor, not Jesus the Victim. He can identify with our weaknesses and sorrows and temptation, *but*

---

6. H. N. Ridderbos, "The General Character of Paul's Preaching of Christ," *Paul and Jesus* (Nutley, New Jersey: Presbyterian and Reformed, 1977), 69.

He cannot identify with us in defeat — only in victory. He can no longer identify with the three Hebrew boys who might perish in the fire; He can only identify with three Hebrew boys who are victorious over the fire.

Your way of thinking and mine must be dominated daily by this one fact — the Lord we love and serve is the Risen Lord, the Lord of victory and power and hope and joy and transformation. There is no other Lord.

Jesus is incapable of commiserating with a life of defeat. He can only lead us from defeat to victory. *Jesus knows no other way.*

Too many Christians live as though Jesus is still buried in the ground. But that Jesus is gone forever. There is no other Jesus to love and serve. *The Risen Lord is the only Lord there is.* The victorious Lord is only Lord there is. The joyous Lord is the only Lord there is. The powerful Lord is only Lord there is.

It is *this* Lord to Whom we are united.

Paul's point: we can live the Christian life only by union with *this* Jesus, not the Jesus of Bethlehem or Nazareth or even Golgotha, but the Jesus of the empty tomb.

Therefore, according to Paul, *there is no other Christian life possible except the life of victory and joy and power and hope and worldwide transformation* (1 Cor. 15:56-58; 1 Jn. 5:4).

This is the Risen Jesus Whom we serve, **and there is simply no other Jesus**.

CHAPTER 7

Unction: The Missing Element

Christianity takes for granted the absence of any self-help
and offers a power which is nothing less than the power
of God. This power is to come upon powerless men as
a gentle but resistless invasion from another world
bringing a moral potency infinitely beyond anything that
might be stirred up from within. This power is sufficient;
no additional help is needed, no auxiliary source of
spiritual energy, for it is the Holy Spirit of God come
where the weakness lay to supply power and grace to
meet the moral need.

A. W. Tozer, *"The Spirit Is Power"*[1]

If I had the space, I could address many problems in today's church and in Christianity. I could highlight the doctrinal downright absurdity of a willingness to believe in anything or nothing and still call this belief Christian. I could explore the ubiquitous moral laxity — fornication, adultery, even controversy over whether homosexuals should be ordained to the Gospel ministry. I could discuss the seeker-sensitive fad — reconfiguring the church to conform to what the unrepentant desire in a church. I could, in addition, note the entertainment religion — the "feel-good Jesus" that leaps to our every beck and call. I could, moreover, document the lovelessness and divisiveness among individuals who are committed to the love of truth, but not the *truth of love*, perhaps the most important truth of all. I could go on and on.

Nonetheless, for some odd reason — I am tempted to say a sinister or diabolical reason — one acute problem always seems to escape our attention. That problem is utter powerlessness, lack of any mention of the loss of the power of the Holy Spirit in the

---

1. *A Treasury of A. W. Tozer* (Harrisburg, Pennsylvania: Christian Publications, 1980), 58.

church. He is the absent One, and most pernicious of all, we seem not to miss His absence.

Powerless lives seem the routine: churches go through the motions of churchianity without ever experiencing the sweet breath of heaven that should energize all they do.   Parents train their children without once thinking of the Holy Spirit.   Husbands and wives desire successful Christian marriages and seem convinced that they can obtain the blessing of God apart from the power of the Holy Spirit.   Churches are well-oiled machines — extensive motion, but no power.   The culture drifts into depravity as Christians try to change its politics; but they have not learned the lesson that the Holy Spirit alone changes cultures, nothing less. Apart from the Pentecostals and Charismatics, there is often a nearly absolute blind spot when it comes to the presence and power of the Holy Spirit in today's church.[2]

Of this omission it is crucial to recognize one fact: *it has nothing to do with the Faith we actually see in the Bible.*   In the Bible, where the Holy Spirit is at work, *there is power.*

The Holy Spirit's Power in the Bible

We encounter it prominently in Acts chapter 1, Luke's sequel of his gospel. There, Luke tells us what Jesus did while on earth, and then in Acts, he writes the sequel. In other words, the work of Jesus did not end when Jesus ascended to heaven. In John 14-16, Jesus had alerted His disciples that He must go away. Of course, they loved Him, so they are saddened by this revelation. "We've given our lives to this Messiah. All of our hopes and dreams and salvation are invested in Him. And now He's leaving?" You can imagine how heartbroken they were. But He comforts them by saying that they will not be alone. Indeed, he makes a strange promise. He assures them, "I must go, but I'll send Someone else." And that Someone else is the Holy Spirit. Likewise, in John 16:7 Jesus utters a staggering statement — to these disciples, these men

---

2. John R. Rice, *The Power of Pentecost* (Murfreesboro, Tennessee: Sword of the Lord Publishers, 1949).

who have left all previous entanglements to follow Him — He says, "It's to your advantage that I leave." Their advantage? How can that be? Is it really preferable for them for Jesus to be gone? Yes, Jesus declares, "Because I'm sending another Comforter, another Helper. And you can't imagine the work that this Guy can do." Of course, He denotes the Holy Spirit. Do we understand that Jesus said that *it is preferable for the Holy Spirit to be with us than for Jesus Himself to be with us physically?*[3] That assertion suggests how important the Holy Spirit is.

The Holy Spirit comes in an unprecedented way at that first post-resurrection Pentecost. And Luke makes clear what He supplies: *power.*[4] The disciples were to be witnesses of Jesus' resurrection, declaring His Gospel and Lordship to the whole world (Acts 1:1-8). No doubt their hearts were brimming with enthusiasm to tell their countrymen about this Galilean that had died and risen and was in heaven ruling on David's throne. But Jesus told them, "Don't do it. First, make sure the Holy Spirit arrives in power. Wait for the promise."

We may deduce from this assertion that the *preaching of the Gospel to the world will be ineffectual apart from the mighty baptizing power of the Holy Spirit.*[5] If we want to know why the declaration of the Gospel is often ineffectual, I would submit that we lack the power of the Holy Spirit. But it is prevalent — brimming over — in the book of Acts. In Acts 2 the Spirit comes as a great rushing wind and tongues of fire. The most significant factor about this staggering event was not the speaking in tongues and the cloven tongues that sat on each of the believers: these phenomena were results. The significant factor was the arrival of the Holy Spirit in massive, unprecedented power.

Similarly, in Acts 4 Peter stands before the Sanhedrin to give

---

3. Leon Morris, *The Gospel According to John* (Grand Rapids: Eerdmans, 1971), 696-697.
4. Alan Richardson, *An Introduction to the Theology of the New Testament* (London: SCM Press, 1958), 111.
5. On the power of the Holy Spirit in Gospel proclamation, see John Murray, "The Power of the Holy Spirit," *Collected Writings of John Murray* (Edinburgh: Banner of Truth, 1976), 1:138-142.

account for the healing of the lame man. We read (v. 8) that he was filled with the Holy Spirit — and he spoke the Gospel with great boldness to these enemies of Jesus. This from the apostle that three times denied Jesus and cursed Him with an oath. What had changed? The presence of the power of the Holy Spirit. The Holy Spirit's power is incompatible with timidity.

In v. 31, after the believers had joined together in great, bold prayer, we read that the place where they were assembled was shaken (a sensory expression of power), and all of them were filled with the Holy Spirit, and they spoke the Word with great boldness.

In Acts 9:17, we read that Ananias laid his hands on Paul, after Paul was converted, and he prayed that God would heal Paul's blindness and fill him with the Holy Spirit. And then in Acts 13, we read that Paul was in Cyprus and was filled with the Holy Spirit and we read of the great *power* in his preaching and life. (Would you like to know why the Gospel got to you? Because about 2000 years ago the first Gentile missionary was filled with the Holy Spirit in great power.)

This power does not refer to the indwelling of the Spirit that happens when we are regenerated (Eph. 4:3). Everyone trusting Jesus has the Holy Spirit's indwelling, but not all are filled, anointed, baptized, and sealed in the Spirit in great power.[6] Not all Christians, therefore, possess the power of the Holy Spirit.

Nonetheless, as Gordon Fee has pointed out, the Holy Spirit is God's presence in the world today.[7] His presence has replaced the presence of Jesus, Who is ruling in heaven. God is here in the Person of the Holy Spirit.

Unfortunately, some of our theologians and preachers, who seemingly would not know the Holy Spirit's power if it punched them in the face, assure us that the Holy Spirit's power we encoun-

---

6. Martyn Lloyd-Jones, *Joy Unspeakable* (Wheaton: Harold Shaw, 1984), 157. This book is bathed in an experiential knowledge of the power of the Spirit and serves as a stinging rebuke to the scholastic powerlessness of much of the modern conservative church — conservative to a fault.

7. Gordon Fee, *Paul, the Spirit and the People of God* (Peabody, Massachusetts: Hendrickson Publications, 1996), 15f.

ter in the Bible was limited to the apostolic age. It is imperative
to recognize that if this opinion is valid, the church cannot fulfill
the Great Commission, cannot evangelize the world; and cannot
expect great Gospel victory,[8] *because the commission of the Gospel is*
predicated on the power of the presence of the Holy Spirit.[9]

A prime example of the assault on the doctrine of the Holy
Spirit's great, powerful anointing is Daniel R. Hyde.[10] Hyde warns
against seeking the power and joy of the Holy Spirit apart from
the Sunday morning preaching of the Word and the sacraments,
which to him seem the exclusive vehicles for experiencing the
Spirit. He domesticates the Spirit in the hands of Christian minis-
ters who may then, apparently, manipulate Him. Hyde concludes
his article: "Are you in search of the Holy Spirit but can't seem
to find what you are looking for? Search no longer. There is no
need to continue trying to find the Spirit in direct experience upon
the soul of the believer, as Pente-costalism [*sic*], mysticism, and
pietism teach. Instead, you can experience his presence in public
worship — as that is his place of residence — by hearing his voice
in the preaching of the gospel and coming into contact with his
grace and power in the sacraments." The fact that no one in the
New Testament talked that way — or could possibly have talked
that way or even thought to talk that way — seems not to have occurred to Hyde.

If we cannot have the power of the Book of Acts, we cannot
have the Commission of the Book of the Acts, so intertwined were
the two.

---

8. John Jefferson Davis, *Christ's Victorious Kingdom* (Grand Rapids: Baker, 1986).

9. I disagree with Richard B. Gaffin Jr. that the first post-resurrection Pentecost was a
non-repeatable, redemptive-historical event within the complex that includes the resurrection and ascension of Jesus. See his "Challenges of the Charismatic Movement to
the Reformed Tradition," *Proceedings of the International Conference of Reformed Churches,*
October 15-23, 1997 Seoul, Korea (Neerlandia, Alberta, Canada: Inheritance Publications,
1997), 171, n. 26. It is clear to me that the power of the Spirit and its evidences un-
leashed at that event recurred in the New Testament era and were meant, at times, to
accompany Gospel preaching in the present church era subsequent to the redemptive-
historical era.

10. Daniel R. Hyde, "In Search of the Spirit," *Modern Reformation*, July/August 2008,
23-26.

But while it came in fullness only *then*, that power did not begin at that momentous Pentecost.

Power of the Holy Spirit in the Old Testament

In Judges 14:6, for instance, we read that a young lion confronted Samson, and the Holy Spirit came mightily on him and he ripped the lion in pieces with his bare hands as one would a young goat. In 1 Samuel 16 we read that at his anointing at the hands of Samuel, the Holy Spirit rushed upon David mightily. In Micah 3:8, the prophet declares that he is able to rebuke the sins of Israel by the filling of the power of the Spirit of the Lord.

What of our Lord? In Luke 4:14 we read, "And Jesus returned in the *power of the Spirit* into Galilee: and there went out a fame of him through all the region round about." When he first stood in the synagogue to preach, He quoted Isaiah, "The Spirit of the Lord is on me." *Jesus was a Spirit-filled preacher.* Likewise Paul. We read in 1 Corinthians 2:4, "And my speech and my preaching [was] not with enticing words of man's wisdom, but in demonstration of the *Spirit and of power*."

There's a word not used much these days. Many Christians from the 19th century knew it — and they experienced it. Many moderns (and postmoderns) do not know the word, and they apparently do not experience it, either. The older word is **unction**, a basic synonym for "anointing." It connotes *power*. Almost nobody talks about it today. Almost nobody prays for it today. Almost nobody cares about it today. *And these omissions show.*

Preaching is reduced to a bare intellectualism or a blathering emotionalism.[11] The Sunday gathering is a glorified social club, or an entertainment center, or a lecture hall, or a liturgical performance — anything but a people empowered by the Holy Spirit and enjoying His sweet breath. There are reasons for this loss.

Some Christians are afraid to talk of the Holy Spirit because of the embarrassing beliefs and activities occurring in the name of

---

11. For a healthy corrective, see Roger Wagner, *Tongues Aflame* (Geanies House, Fearn, Tain, Ross-shire, England, 2004).

the Holy Spirit: the laughing revival, barking dogs, and so on. We cannot, however, allow excesses to drive us away from the truth. We read in the Bible that those who persecute Jesus' followers will think they're doing God a service (Jn. 16:2). Do we quit following the God of heaven and earth on the grounds that some people murder in His name? Of course not. We expose the perversion and persist in following the Lord. Similarly, we must not quit craving the Holy Spirit's power just because some people have succumbed to absurdity. We cannot serve the King effectively — whether in school, family, vocation, culture, politics, and church — without the power of the Holy Spirit.

Getting the Power

How do we obtain it? Clearly God refuses to fill those who are in willful sin. If we grieve or quench the Holy Spirit, we cannot expect His power (Eph. 4:30; 1 Thes. 5:19). God removed His Spirit from King Saul for His presumptuous sin. So, if one is in a state of intentional, unconfessed sin, he cannot expect the power of the Spirit.

While theories abound as to how one elicits the power of the Holy Spirit, Luke 11:13 furnishes a clue: "If ye then, being evil, know how to give good gifts unto your children: how much more shall [your] heavenly Father give the Holy **Spirit** to them that **ask** him?" Why are so many Christians powerless? Why do they live lives of protracted ineffectiveness? Why are churches so boring and status quo? They never ask God for the Holy Spirit. So God doesn't give Him. *If we're content not to have the Holy Spirit's power, God is often content not to give Him.*

May it never be said of us that the Holy Spirit is absent from our lives and churches simply because He hasn't been *invited*. That would be a tragedy. Let us pray for the mighty filling and power of the Holy Spirit, so that God would be glorified, souls would be saved, the sick would be healed, Christians would gain great victory over besetting sin — and that God's kingdom would extend throughout the entire earth. It'll never happen without the Holy Spirit — He is God's presence in the world.

Jack Carter is the long-time pastor of Church of the King in Corpus Christi. His church meeting on Sunday is bathed in the presence and power of the Spirit. I once asked him, "Jack, what's the secret?" He replied, "Well, we decided long ago never to be in hurry. We wait on the Spirit. We don't demand that He get on our timetable; we try to get on His timetable. We want for the Spirit." *The Spirit is worth waiting for.*

Christians will never accomplish great things in the church or outside its bounds without **unction** — without the power of the Holy Spirit.

CHAPTER 8

Contra Compartmentalization

*The faith-reason division of the medieval era and the
religion-science division of the early modern era had
become one of subject-object, inner-outer, man-world,
humanities-science. A new form of the double-truth
universe was now established.*

Richard Tarnas, *The Passion of the Western Mind*[1]

I will address briefly what may well be the single greatest temptation not merely to Christian youth, but to the most extensively and rigorously educated Christian youth of our time, those who have benefited from training and education like they receive at Annapolis Christian Academy. Some historical background is necessary before I disclose that temptation.

The Seeds of Compartmentalization

The world you graduates enter is exceedingly *compartmentalized*. The prime ideational influence on our world is still the 18th century Enlightenment (or "modernism"), which bifurcated human knowledge by banishing religion (mostly Christianity) from the realm of public discourse — and eventually from anywhere except between anybody's two ears.[2] While the medieval world had its problems,[3] including, as this chapter's epigraph notes, a faith-reason split, until Enlightenment it was thought that Christianity was inextricably wedded to culture and that one could not expect to preserve civilization without it. To some degree all of life was

---

1. Richard Tarnas, *The Passion of the Western Mind* (New York: Ballantine, 1991), 376.
2. Peter Gay, *The Enlightenment: The Rise of Modern Paganism* (New York: W. W. Norton, 1966).
3. On Christianity's contribution to the incontestable success of the West, see Rodney Start, *The Victory of Reason* (New York: Random House, 2005).

thought to be religious — notably Christian.[4] The Enlightenment dramatically altered that assumption. Later Enlightenment thinkers saw Christianity as occupying the realm of personal predilection, much as one would prefer decaf to regular coffee. Immanuel Kant, the greatest Enlightenment philosopher of all, essentially banished the Triune God to the realm of the unknowable.[5] In time, "rational people" were convinced that religion was a private matter that should not intrude into the most prominent spheres of life like science and education and economics and business and politics and art. All men were endowed with reason, the standard by which all things were to be judged and a tool by which man could build a world of which his predecessors could only dream. Christianity, which is not anti-reasonable but which is at central points *beyond* reason, tended to impede that dream of reason, so Christianity had no significant place in the later Enlightenment world.

Today, postmodernism (or is it is simply *modern* modernism?) has assaulted the foundation of Enlightenment — its idea of rational objectivity.[6] For this rational objectivity postmodernism has substituted "the positing Self."[7] Man creates his own values (Nietzsche) — in fact, he shapes his own conceptual universe. No longer is there a shared vision of reality in culture — not even the secular, rational vision of reality that the Enlightenment fostered — but rather multiple, competing realities, as many realities as there are people on the planet at any given time. Every person creates his own world.

These waves of, first, Enlightenment and, then, postmodernism have crashed successively on the shore of Western civilization and have begun to erode the very character of its shoreline. Soon, they may wash away its very ideational foundations. The

---

4. Christopher Dawson, *Medieval Essays* (Freeport, New York: Books for Libraries Press, 1954, 1968).
5. Tarnas, *The Passion of the Western Mind*, 341-351.
6. Walter Truett Anderson, *Reality Isn't What It Used to Be* (New York: HarperCollins, 1990).
7. David Wells, *The Courage to Be Protestant* (Grand Rapids: Eerdmans, 2008), ch. 5.

chief manifestation of this erosion (rivaled only by relativism, its twin) is *compartmentalization*. With no single, overarching principle to guide one in life, he or she chops life up into segments, airtight compartments that rarely influence one another.[8] Man's religion does not impact his voting habits; a woman's public morality does not influence her sex life; one's "worldview" does not impinge on how he treats friends and strangers. We know that all individuals carry a worldview, but not all worldviews shape all aspects of life. The chief feature of the postmodern worldview is compartmentalization itself; a worldview that champions worldviews — even competing worldviews — in the life of a single individual.[9] This compartmentalization is standard fare in our world. The unitive individual is a thing of the past.

Public and Private

Political pundits assure us that a key factor in President Bill Clinton's political success was his prowess in compartmentalization, his ability to divide aspects of his life into hermetically sealed, existential compartments. Apparently, at a fund-raising event, he could "lock into" individual donors one at a time, and each was convinced he cared only for that donor. Clinton was supposedly unconcerned with the larger purpose (raising money) and riveted to the needs, desires, and aspirations of the particular individual to whom he was speaking. He could compartmentalize his "private" life from his "public" life. He could carry on illicit sexual relation with a 20-year-old intern, betraying his wife and daughter while (it is asserted) masterfully overseeing a humming economy and domestic tranquility. Different "values" governed different aspects of his life. Much of the American public tended to agree with this assessment, because while many of them believed Clinton

---

8. This divided life is the inheritance of postmodernity's forerunner, Romanticism, which compensated for Enlightenment's supposedly objective rationalism by emphasizing subjective internal aspects of life (like will and emotion) that "objective reason" could not touch. See Harold O. J. Brown, "Romanticism and the Bible," in eds., Gordon Lewis and Bruce Demarest, *Challenges to Inerrancy* (Chicago: Moody, 1984), ch. 2.
9. Wells, *The Courage to Be Protestant*, 110.

was untrustworthy as an individual, they applauded him as their President. The fact that only an *individual* can be President did not seem to occur to them.

Similarly, in an issue of *Time Magazine* some time ago, Lance Morrow argued that the now ninth Circuit Court of Appeals decision that banned the Pledge of Allegiance as unconstitutional was probably wrong; it is permissible to retain "under God" in the Pledge, Morrow suggested, as long as we keep Him out of politics. This is the typical secularist compromise: we may pledge allegiance to a country whose liberties are secured by God's authority, but we many never act on the *reality* of that allegiance, which is, of course, that God (and not our nation) is our ultimate authority. Secularism is essentially a compartmentalization enterprise.[10] It is the notion that Christianity is permitted in the "private" sphere but that it is forbidden in the "public" sphere, "public" meaning the political or the state-funded.

This, incidentally, is one reason that secularists are so eagerly statist and pro-politics: the diminution of the size and scope of the state ordinarily implies the increase of the scope of legitimate religion, because religion (here: Christianity) needs very little of politics to dominate a society; in other words, legitimate religion tends to assume the tasks (education, medicine, economic welfare) that secularists want to reserve to the state alone. I imagine in their most frightening nightmares they envision the possibility of the near abolition of the state — a scenario that may mean, in fact, that religion, and specifically Christianity, would dominate all of life.

Compartmentalized Christianity

The Christian Faith, conversely, does not see man as a compartmentalized being;[11] and it does not see human life, in general,

---

10. Charles Taylor, *A Secular Age* (Cambridge and London: Belknap Press, 2007).

11. I agree with Kevin J. Corcoran that man does not possess an immortal soul, as that term has been used in the Western tradition. See his *Rethinking Human Nature* (Grand Rapids: Baker, 2006).

as compartmentalized. There is an abundance of spheres (for instance, family, church, and state), and there is a division of labor (technology, economics, education, politics, and so forth).[12] But there is no compartmentalization — all of these aspects of human life stand under God's authority mediated in Jesus Christ and communicated in His Word, the Bible.

As thoughtful Christians, therefore, we rightly disdain the principle of compartmentalization; but while disdaining it, we sometimes practice it. The way in which we do this is ironic. We limit our aversion to compartmentalization to the realm of the mind. In short, our opposition to compartmentalization is itself compartmentalized. *This is possibly the single greatest temptation to Christian youth trained in a godly manner in a rigorous academic atmosphere.* The Faith becomes nothing more than a thought system.

Some scholars and theologians, for example, write persuasive tomes exalting God and explicating Biblical truth, but their own lives are in spiritual shambles. They have compartmentalized intellect and reason (particularly "discursive" reason) from the rest of their being. Some Christians, on the other hand, compartmentalize emotion. Emotional intensity (love for God, concern for the unconverted, care for the poor) includes matters of passion but has little to do with intellect or will, with both of which they are little concerned. And what about the will itself? I know of too many Christians for whom the will seems to be a separate compartment. It is somehow not influenced by man's depravity. The center of the Christian life, they believe, is "an act of the will," as though the will could be separated from the total man.

But man is a unified being: his intellect, emotions, and will (and other human factors) subsist together. All of these factors are included in what the Bible calls the "heart."[13] Life, in other words, is holistic, not compartmentalized.

When we compartmentalize, however, it is possible for men

---

12. Abraham Kuyper, "Sphere Sovereignty," in ed., James D. Bratt, *Abraham Kuyper: A Centennial Reader* (Grand Rapids: Eerdmans, 1998), 461-490.
13. Gordon Clark, *Religion, Reason and Revelation* (Jefferson, Maryland: Trinity Foundation, 1986), 92.

to argue violently for Christian education (in opposition to public education) while playing fast and loose with pornography. When we compartmentalize, we demand Christian influence in politics but not Christian influence over our tongue, which engages in gossip and tale bearing and divisiveness. When we compartmentalize, women pontificate about the need for a "Christian worldview" while mistreating their husband or caring nothing for unbelievers. If we compartmentalize, it is possible to engage in the most heinous sins while maintaining the most pristine Christian profession. *But aversion to compartmentalization cannot itself be compartmentalized.* We must oppose compartmentalization with every aspect of our being, not merely the intellect.

Some older theologians would refer to the "religious affections," the deepest desires of our heart for God. Likewise, A. W. Tozer once wrote, "We are becoming what we love."[14] The words are weighty, and we do well to ponder them. If our Faith is merely a matter of intellectual assent or moral rectitude or compelling scholarship or church machinery, we are guilty of compartmentalization. And the effects of that compartmentalization will be exhibited in our lives. Entire areas of our lives will be immune from the authority of Jesus Christ and the power of the Holy Spirit.

But to one who is imbued with a love for God, one who is passionate in his affection for Jesus Christ, one who says from the heart, "Jesus is mine and I am His; I love Him with every fiber of my being," there is simply no room for compartmentalization. We live all of life to the glory of Jesus Christ because we cannot do otherwise: our entire being is imbued with passion to please Him. He is not just our Lord and Savior but also our Friend and constant Companion. He dominates our thinking and our actions our entire waking hours — and even our sleep.

Conclusion

Our great calling in our individual lives, families, churches,

14. A. W. Tozer, "We Are Becoming What We Love," *God Tells the Man Who Cares* (Bromley, Kent, England: STL Books, 1980), 156-163.

and the wider society is to break down the walls of contemporary compartmentalization that seal off certain aspects of life from
our Lord's authority and our passion for Him. We must inculcate
in our children that Jesus Christ is Lord of all things, not simply
Sunday church, family devotions, their prayer closets, and their
sex lives. The church speaks authoritatively not only on issues
like the Trinity and the resurrection but also gene splicing and
preemptive war and immigration and special quotas for homosexuals. Christian politics must not refuse to address issues simply because they are considered "moral" or "religious." *Of course*,
they are moral and religious. What other kinds of issues are there?
Rightly or wrongly, all legislation from speed limits to tax rates to
bankruptcy proceedings spring from a moral, that is to say *religious*,
premise.

But, more pointedly and relevantly, our Faith is not only an
intellectual postulate.[15] It must pervade every fiber of our being.
Jesus asserted that the great demand of God on man is to love Him
with our heart, soul, strength and mind (Mt. 22:37; Lk. 10:27).
Christianity is not an ideology.[16] It generates a worldview, but it is
not a worldview. It cannot be reduced to a way of thinking, even
a compelling, comprehensive way of thinking. It is at root a deep,
profound, personal relationship with Jesus Christ that reorients
sinful man to the core of his being. It transforms man from the
inside out. It compels us to love Jesus Christ with such ardor that,
despite our lingering sin, we seek only to please Him in all we do.

I urge you graduates, and all other believers, to renew your
passion and love for Jesus Christ, the One Who died for us and
rose from the dead and lives for us today — the One Whom we
will see and love and commune with throughout eternity.

The advance of Christianization depends to a large measure
on the destruction of compartmentalization. And the advance

---

15. On the vital role of the intellect in the Christian life, see Harold O. J. Brown, "The
Conservative Option," in eds., Stanley N. Gundry and Alan F. Johnson, *Tensions in
Contemporary Theology* (Chicago: Moody Press, 1979 edition), 438-443.
16. P. Andrew Sandlin, "Faith versus Ideology," in ed., Steven M. Schlissel, *The Standard
Bearer* (Nacogdoches, Texas: Covenant Media, 2002), 309-317.

of your own sanctification depends on assuring a devotion to the Person of Jesus Christ that pervades every aspect of your being.

Let us work tirelessly to de-compartmentalize our lives and all of society.

CHAPTER 9

Western Philosophy: Christian versus Classical

[T]he genius of Christianity is the reversal of the genius of the Greeks.

Cornelius Van Til, *A Survey of Christian Epistemology*[1]

We often use the term *philosophy* as shorthand for a set of basic concepts underlying a discipline, as in "A Christian *philosophy* of education" or "Her *philosophy* of life is hedonistic." However, in this talk, unless otherwise expressed, I denote by *philosophy* the Western tradition of the preeminent thinkers about ultimate issues, from metaphysics to existence to truth to reality to freedom to duty. I refer, therefore, to the tradition from the pre-Socratics in ancient Greece right down to Richard Rorty and John Searle in the modern world. Philosophy, therefore, means this tradition of these leading thinkers who have deeply influenced the West.

As Christians we assess this philosophy from the standpoint of our distinctive presuppositions. We can't address philosophy in a vacuum, for there aren't, in fact, any vacuums in the realm of ideas. But even to make this assertion is to leap into a philosophical controversy. Can we encounter objects of knowledge (and an idea is surely an object of knowledge) in an "objective" way uninfluenced by our own historical milieu, our emotional state, and even our physiology? This is a question for philosophy. At the very outset, then, we observe an important fact — in discussing ultimate issues of life, and in discussing *how* to discuss them, we have already entered the realm of philosophy. This is no less true of Christians than of everybody else.

It is true that some Christians have decried the influence

---

1. (Phillipsburg, New Jersey: Presbyterian and Reformed, n.d.), 24.

of philosophy on Christianity, particularly on theology. This was the view of "crisis" theologian Karl Barth. Yet Barth was profoundly influenced by existentialism, especially in his early years.[2] Cornelius Van Til was trained in philosophical idealism at Princeton; and while he opposed idealism as such, it's clear that idealism influenced his "presuppositional" apologetic method.[3] Similarly, anyone who has read the simple, clear, plain theology of Greg Bahnsen and John Frame detects that each was trained in the analytic method of philosophy, which prizes just such direct, unadorned communication.[4] So, even if only in methodology, we cannot fully escape philosophical influences.

Trying to write theology purged of any philosophic influence is like trying to change a flat tire without a jack. You must have tools for the job. Philosophy furnishes (among other things) the conceptual tools of theology. The same goes for education and teaching. The very methods we employ (not to mention our view of knowledge and how it is attained) betray a commitment to some school or schools of philosophy, whether we know it or not. The question is *how* we will appropriate philosophy, not *whether* we will appropriate it.

Tonight, my main objective is modest: to suggest that, with rare exception, Biblical Christianity stands at odds with the tradition of Western philosophy, and most notably with its most prominent early source, the classical philosophy of Plato in the ancient world.

Western philosophy springs from an acutely sinful human autonomy first articulated in ancient Greece. For over 2000 years, and until just recently, this classical orientation to philosophy dominated the West. From Plato to Descartes to Marx, it situated man as the measure of all things.[5] Even self-consciously Christian

---

2. Bruce L. McCormack, *Karl Barth's Critically Realistic Dialectical Theology* (Oxford: Oxford University Press, 1995), 216 and *passim*.

3. John M. Frame, *Cornelius Van Til* (Phillipsburg, New Jersey: P & R Publishing, 1995), 21.

4. L[ord] Q[uinton], "Analytic Philosophy," in ed., Ted Honderich, *Oxford Companion to Philosophy* (Oxford: Oxford University Press, 1995), 28-30.

5. Charles S. MacKenzie, "Classical Greek Humanism," in eds., W. Andrew Hoffecker

philosophers like Aquinas and Kierkegaard compromised with the humanism that permeates classical philosophy. This is *the* course of Western philosophy — man, not God, is the measure.

Cornelius Van Til, among others, has drawn attention to the patristic church's compromise with the classical world and its anti-Christian philosophy. The Western church evolved this compromise into a *Biblical-classical* synthesis that undercut the full authority of Jesus Christ speaking authoritatively in the Bible.[6] The Protestant Reformation moved to purge the church of this compromise with classical thought, but it was not entirely successful. Vestiges of classical philosophy lingered.

In the last 300 years Christianity has steadily lost ground as a spiritual force in Western culture. The secularization inherent in a highly developed Western philosophy has emasculated a Christianity that had already at crucial points made its peace with that very philosophy. Christianity has not escaped the bitter fruits of its early compromise with Greek thought — these fruits have now rendered it weak and effete in the face of secularism — and a radical Islam, for that matter.

The recent advent of postmodern (anti-classical) epistemic theories,[7] while posing severe problems of their own, has paved the way for a renewed opportunity for a distinctly Christian approach to philosophy. This "post-foundationalism" denies the myth of an impersonal logos, a rational principle that under girds the universe and thus it opens the way for a reassertion of a highly personal epistemology grounded in the being of Jesus of Nazareth. Further, it sees man as immersed in his culture, not an objective observer, and thus closes all escape routes for those who would short-circuit the created order and the full humanity of man. It moreover recognizes the human (re)construction of knowledge and reality and by this recognition verifies (even if unintentionally) the Creator-

and Gary Scott Smith, *Building a Christian World View* (Phillipsburg, New Jersey: Presbyterian and Reformed, 1986), 1:31-48.

6. Donald G. Bloesch, *A Theology of Word and Spirit* (Downers Grove, Illinois: InterVarsity, 1992), 44-61.

7. David Harvey, *The Condition of Postmodernity* (Oxford: Blackwell, 1990), 4-65.

creature distinction. Of course, secular post-foundationalism, like all secularism, is dangerous,[8] but post-foundationalism does offer possibilities for a resurgence of Biblical Christianity.

In any case, a Christian perspective on philosophy must account for the *Biblical-Hebraic* approach to life and thought and how sharply the *Hellenistic-classical* perspective on philosophy broke with it. I'll briefly sketch some of those differences in this talk.

Suffice it to say, only as we recover the Biblical-Hebraic perspective can we expect to formulate a truly Christian philosophy.

First, though, I'll offer a brief, generic assessment of philosophy from a Christian perspective. There are three prominent characteristics of philosophy that we should bear in mind.

Characteristics of Philosophy

First, philosophy is *rational*. Philosophy is primarily about the life of the mind. From Plato onward, philosophers have wanted to get rid of superstition and to subordinate life to human reason. Some have held a higher view of reason than others (for Nietzsche and Heidegger, for example, reason was less important). But almost all Western philosophers believe that the human mind is a powerful instrument that may and must be used to judge reality. By their very nature, philosophers are *thinkers*. There are no "dumb" philosophers. They may hold "dumb" ideas, but they are not "dumb" individuals. They think, and they think hard. And they usually hold an exalted view of human reason. Western philosophy, then, is *rational*.

Second, Western philosophy is *abstract*. Philosophers are interested in much more than just common, ordinary living — waking up, getting ready, going to work, getting married, spending money, and so on. They like to step back from the concrete aspects of life and think about ultimate meaning. When they do this, they naturally develop *abstraction*. For instance, in Plato we read a great deal about justice, friendship, love, freedom, and so forth. Plato,

---

8. Millard J. Erickson, Paul Kjoss Helseth, and Justin Taylor, eds., *Reclaiming the Center* (Wheaton, Illinois: Crossway, 2004).

in fact, created an entire world based on abstraction — the ideal world.

Philosophers aren't just interested in two people who have affection for one another. They want to *abstract* from this relationship the *meaning* of love. What are its characteristics? How does it begin? How does it end? What threatens it? How is it manifested? This means that philosophers oftentimes are not as interested in people *per se* as they are in ideas. In many cases, they believe that real people should conform to abstract ideas, rather than the other way around.

For example, V.I. Lenin, though not technically a philosopher, was heavily influenced by the philosopher Karl Marx. In his revolutionary regime in Russia, hundreds of thousands were murdered. Yet, Lenin was largely unmoved by the horrors going on daily around him.[9] He was more interested in economic programs and abstract statistics on a page that were delivered to him every afternoon. Flesh-and-blood people were mostly unimportant to him. What was important was how the people fulfilled certain abstract ideas.

Of course, most Western philosophers aren't as heartless as Lenin. However, they do tend to give great emphasis to the abstract. They live within the world of the mind. Philosophy is *abstract*.

Third, and perhaps more importantly, Western philosophy is *humanistic*. With rare exception, Western philosophers see man as the measure of all things. In fact, one of the great objectives of Western philosophy is to liberate man from the tyranny of God and religions and superstitions. This is most evident in Immanuel Kant, who defined the Enlightenment as man's emancipation from his own self-imposed slavery to traditional authorities like God, the Bible, the church, and so on.[10] But almost all Western philosophers hold this view to one degree or another. Many philosophers

9. Richard Pipes, *Communism — A History* (New York: Modern Library, 2001), ch. 2.
10. John Jefferson Davis, "Kant and the Problem of Religious Knowledge," in eds., Kenneth S. Kantzer and Stanley N. Gundry, *Perspectives in Evangelical Theology* (Grand Rapids: Baker, 1979), 231-250.

claimed to be Christians, but, on the whole, their philosophy wasn't grounded in the Bible. We think immediately of Descartes and Locke. Even the philosophers who ostensibly tried to honor God, like Aquinas and Kierkegaard, went seriously astray. Philosophy puts man at the center. When you do that, you erode and eventually destroy the Christian Faith, which is *theocentric*.

But this is precisely what Western philosophy has done. It has contributed to the compromise and decimation of the Christian Faith. Greek philosophy influenced the Church Fathers. Aristotle's philosophy plagued the medieval Church's doctrine. Enlightenment philosophy destroyed Protestant orthodoxy. On the whole, Western philosophy is an enemy of the Christian Faith.

Much of that philosophy has been in the classical mode, that is, it has been heavily shaped by ancient Hellenic thought. And of the classical philosophers, none has been more influential than Plato. He is the fountainhead of classical philosophy and its broad tenets. Plato, even more than Socrates and Aristotle, is *the* central ancient philosopher. In fact, although there were philosophers before him (the pre-Socratics), and although there was wide diversity in ancient philosophy, Plato really set Western philosophy moving forward. His own philosophy would influence the Western tradition for over two thousand years. Plato's philosophy was *rationalistic*. It was *abstract*. And it was *humanistic*. In these ways and others, it's had an acute influence not only on Western philosophy, but also on Western culture and the church. Tonight I am interested mostly in its influence on Christianity and the church. First, however, a quick survey of some of Plato's leading philosophical tenets.[11]

The World of the Forms or Ideas

If you understand nothing else about Plato's views, you need to know his most important view. This is his doctrine of the Forms or Ideas. To grasp this better, you need to get a sense of why he

---

11. For a fine introduction, consult the multi-author entry "Plato and Platonism" in *The New Encyclopedia Britannica* (Chicago: University of Chicago Press, 1988, 15th edition), 25:880-887.

thought this mighty abstraction was necessary.

More than about anything else, the ancient Greeks feared disorder and chaos. They had suffered from deprivations of war and the violence of anarchy. They saw the world as constantly changing, and this fact frightened them. Above all else, they wanted order, immutability, and permanence. Plato developed (or, rather, refined) an ingenious theory to solve this problem.

Plato believed that the physical world in which we live is not the *real* world. The real world stands behind this material world. (In this sense, he was what we nowadays call an idealist.) The *real* world is the world of the Forms and Ideas. He used his famous parable of the cave to describe it.

Imagine, if you will (Plato suggested) almost all of humanity sequestered in a large, underground cave. Everybody in it is chained, and facing one wall. They are restrained in such a way that they cannot turn their head. They can only look at one large wall. Behind them is a lighted fire. That fire is the only light in the cave. In front of that fire, but still to the back of the chained people, is a little path. Along this path, certain individuals carry objects, figures of men and animals and all sorts of other things that, due to the light, project an image onto the wall at which the chained individuals are looking.

Now, Plato enquires, what would the individuals who are chained think of all of this? Well, he responds, since they didn't know anything else, they would presume that these images cast on the wall were, in fact, life's *reality*. Because they never saw what real people looked like, the only "people" they knew were the shadows on the wall. And this is true of everything else they knew.

Well, Plato suggested, this is the way the present world works. The shadows and images cast on the cave wall are the sense experiences of this present, material world. These images are not the real world; they are only an imperfect representation of the real world that stands behind them.

For example, we look at a chair. This chair is an imperfect image of the ideal, eternal chair in the real world that we cannot see. All chairs participate in this Form or Idea of "chairness." A big goal is to try to make chairs in this world as close as possible to the chair of the ideal world.

But Plato wasn't concerned most of all with chairs. He was interested in Ideas or Forms, such as Beauty or Justice. There is a perfection of these ideas in the spiritual, higher, *real* world. In the present world, we try (with our reason) to discover what these eternal ideas are and to implement them. The things of the present world are only imperfect forms or copies of the ideal. This is true of man as well. There is the Ideal Man, and we must work to try to become (or create) him.

Now, this theory may sound fanciful or even goofy to you, but it's exactly what Plato — and many others — believed.

Tripartite View of Man

The second of Plato's chief ideas is his tripartite view of man. Plato taught that man consists of three parts: reason, spirit (or will), and appetite. Now remember that, for the most part, Plato was a rationalist. Plato believed that reason is the core, and most important, part of man.

Then there is the spirit, or will. This is the part of man that leads to and creates action.

Then there are the appetites. These can sometimes be good, but they usually are bad. Appetites, of course, would include food and sex.

Now Plato believed that reason should govern everything. Reason should govern our will, and our will, in turn, should govern our appetites. Part of the world's problems, he suggested, is that men are ruled by appetites rather than by reason. This is why they live in debauchery.

This is also why Plato wanted a highly rationalistic ethics. His ethics were not anything close to Christian, of course. For example, he wasn't inherently opposed to homosexuality. Many of the "enlightened" Greeks and Romans taught that homosexuality was a "higher" form of ethics. The main thing is that ethics were to be demonstrated by reason, not by some religion or superstition or outside force.

Consequently, Plato often set forth his views in the form

of a dialogue. He would recount a narrative of individuals surrounding a wise teacher — usually Socrates. He would put words
into their mouths as they pursued some topic. "What is justice?"
Socrates may ask. And then, little by little, he would elicit answers
from his followers. He would gently show where he believed they
were wrong, and then, after a while, he would lead them to his
(correct) conclusions.

To Plato, the most important thing a man could achieve is
the idea of Good. Remember: this is an idea; it is not inherent in
the present world. We must strive through reason to discover it
and then to implement it.

Man, therefore, should be in a constant battle with himself,
beating down his appetite and even his will and submitting them
to his reason.

Knowledge as Recollection

This exaltation of reason is possible because of another cor-
nerstone in Plato's thought — knowledge as recollection. Not
surprisingly, Plato didn't have a very high regard for sense experience. Rather, he was close to a pure rationalist — there are "in-
nate ideas." That is, people are *born* with certain ideas — in fact,
even before birth they possess something of a knowledge of the *real*
world, the world of Ideas and Forms.

Plato believed that the soul is the *real* part of man and that it
is not only eternal but also preexistent. The soul exists pre-tempo-
rally, and at birth, it "gets" a body. According to Plato, this is not a
very good thing. Why? Because then the reason is subjected to the
appetite and the changeable world and human history. And these
tend to undermine reason. In other words, if men were not within
history, and not subjected to their body and all of its appetites,
they could think quite clearly. But they're plagued by desires for
food and sex, by all of the changes of life going on around them.
Therefore, they often cannot reason very effectively. This factor
leads directly to the final distinctive of Plato's thought.

Devaluation of the Body, the Material World and Human

History

Since the body and the present life interfere with reason, quite naturally, a great objective of life is to get rid of the body and history. Therefore, Plato's approach toward the present life is essentially escapist. The true philosopher, in fact, lusts for death. Socrates, for instance, was quite happy to die. Death was the great release. His soul could fly into the world of Forms and Ideas. He would then have perfect reason, perfect understanding. He would no longer be plagued with the appetites and all of the changes that occur in the present life. He would be timeless, eternal, immortal.

Plato, therefore, like many of the ancient Greeks, was a strong advocate of the immortality of the soul. At death, the body is corrupted and goes back to the ground, but the soul, which predated the body, will also survive it. In other words, the body and the present life are sort of a parenthesis in the unending sentence of man's soul. Man's soul didn't have a beginning, and it won't have an end. But the body has both a beginning and an end. This present life is simply an unfortunate phase that the soul has to endure.

These are some of the leading tenets of Plato's philosophy.

Now, it is crucial to grasp that Biblical Christianity is *at every major point* in direct conflict with Platonism and much Greek philosophy. Further, it seems as though certain teachings of the New Testament are almost designed to *refute* that philosophy, which was prominent in the Roman Empire at the time. Biblical Christianity has virtually nothing to do with Greek philosophy. And the extent to which Greek philosophy is imported into Christianity is the extent to which it loses its distinctiveness and becomes almost another religion altogether.

Platonism in Christianity

We will return to this fact in a moment. But now let's ask: How influential is Platonism in today's world? The interesting answer is, not as much as you might expect. It has greatly influenced the Western world up until the last two centuries or so, but today there's a strong aversion to Platonism and Greek philosophy. As a matter of fact, Platonism has lost influence in the modern world in the face of post-foundationalism and postmodernism. It does survive in the revival of philosophy among the Roman Catholics and even the Reformed, but its influence in the culture has been greatly diminished.

There is a single, glaring exception. *Platonism still deeply affects the church and Christianity.* This influence started very early. Some of the early apologists for the Faith were quite educated, and they believed that the Faith must be intelligently defended. The most intellectually respectable defense they knew was Platonism, so they fused Platonism and other expressions of Greek philosophy onto Christianity. This was especially true in the Eastern Church, but it also occurred in the West. Augustine, for example, was obviously influenced by Plato.[12]

Down to the present day, Platonic and Greek ideas have infected the church. This doesn't imply that they are supported by the Bible. In fact, the Bible implicitly refutes them.

Therefore, if we are to recover a Biblical Faith, we must *repudiate* Hellenic and classical thinking in the church and Christianity. How has Platonism in particular affected the Faith?

Flawlessness and Timelessness within History

Well, let's begin with the Forms and Ideas. The patristic church looked for a sort of idealized Faith that stood at the forefront of classical thinking. Because many Christians are looking for absolute, timeless perfection in this life, they are constantly creating eternal Forms and Ideas by which to judge the imperfections (real or perceived) in the present world. I'm not referring to Jesus Christ, Who is of course sinless, nor to the Bible, which is God's infallible Word. Rather, I refer to a lust for perfection within history that drinks deeply at Plato's well.

An "invisible" church? An example: Some people have

---

12. Jaroslav Pelikan, *The Emergence of the Catholic Tradition* (Chicago and London: University of Chicago Press, 1971), 292-307.

taken the idea of the "invisible church" to such an extreme that they refuse to be a member of any actual, local church. The "invisible church" is akin to Plato's timeless Forms, and church historians detect Platonism behind the patristic church's adoption of the "invisible church." How? It exists only in the mind of God. It's never reachable in this life. It is a standard by which we judge these poor, imperfect churches down here. The problem is simply this: the Bible does not teach it. There's no "invisible church" in the Bible.[13] There surely is an invisible *dimension* to the church,[14] if by this we mean a church as God sees it. But, of course, we cannot see things as God sees them, certainly not in the *sense* in which He sees them. The "invisible church" is allegedly made up of all truly elect believers. But we do not know who the elect are, and who the elect are not, and they are never in any "invisible" church anywhere at any time.

Some churches develop schemes by which to ferret out those who are saved and those who are not. But nobody in the Bible does this. It's true that there are unbelievers in the church and, in fact, that the church may be replete with non-Christians. Yet Jesus said that the harvest must grow until the Final Day, and then He — and He alone — will separate the wheat from the chaff. We are called to operate in the sphere of the present world. But this means putting up with very sinful people — including very sinful pastors and elders. It means the church will always have problems of some sort. The church is filled with finite and sinful people. There is no ideal "invisible church" to which we can flee. We cannot say, "Well, we'll leave this sinful, earthly church, and we won't align ourselves with any church, because we're members of the single 'Invisible Church.'" The Bible simply knows of no such thing. You're either a member of the church down here, or you're

13. John Murray, "The Church: Its Definition in Terms of 'Visible and 'Invisible' Invalid," *Collected Writings of John Murray* (Edinburgh, Scotland: Banner of Truth, 1976), 1:231-236.
14. John Murray, *Christian Baptism* (Phillipsburg, New Jersey: Presbyterian and Reformed, 1980), 31-33. For an equally balanced treatment, see Douglas Wilson, "The Church: Visible or Invisible," in ed., Steve Wilkins and Duane Garner, *The Federal Vision* (Monroe, Louisiana: Athanasius Press, 2004), ch. 8.

not a member of the church. I'm not suggesting that if you're not a member of a Church, you're not a Christian. Only God knows that. *And that's the point!* Only those who are members of the church can be considered Christians. We don't claim to play God and know some alleged Forms and Ideas. We only claim to be faithful to the revelation God has given us.

Creaturely theology. Now there is another example of this Platonic error in the Church. It's in the area of theology. Good theology is godly men's reflections on God's revelation in the Bible. The Bible is God's infallible Word. But man's theology is not infallible.[15] Good theology is like good preaching — it is valuable and it should be heeded, but it is not infallible.

However, we do have some folks who seem to think that their theology is akin to a Platonic Form. They consider it timeless, unchangeable, and virtually unrevisable.[16] This is a form of theological idolatry. As Christians, we must believe in the authority of Jesus Christ, and as Protestants we must believe in the *Sola Scriptura.* Nobody writes timeless, unchangeable theology.

Recognizing this fact drags us down from our halo-encircled heads in the clouds and brings us back to the faithful work in the church in time and history. We all speak from a different perspective — even God inspired the New Testament gospels from different perspectives of the human authors.[17] We hold to the ecumenical creeds and Reformation confessions, not because they are the infallible Word of God, but because the church (or at least our sector of it) has made a definitive statement about it/them.

The work of theology is ongoing. Theology has to meet new cultural situations and attacks all the time. The Bible is unchangeable and unchanging, but history and culture changes, and this is why we need new theologies in every generation.[18] There is no

---

15. James Brown, *Subject and Object in Modern Theology* (London: SCM Press, 1955), 12.

16. Francis Pieper, *Christian Dogmatics* (St. Louis: Concordia, 1950), 51-52.

17. Vern S. Poythress, *Symphonic Theology* (Phillipsburg, New Jersey: P & R Publishing, 1987, 2001), 49.

18. Clark H. Pinnock, "Prospects for Systematic Theology," in eds., Clark H. Pinnock and David F. Wells, *Toward a Theology for the Future* (Carol Stream, Illinois: Creation

sort of ideal, timeless Form of theology.

There are so many more examples of this lust for perfection and timelessness and immutability in this life, but I'll leave it at that.

Diminution of Creation

Next, Plato and Greek philosophy and much of the classical world have bequeathed to the church a dreadful view of creation. Historically orthodox Christians believe that God is the good Creator, Who created all things just as He intended. However, sin entered, and the creation is cursed because of sin. But the creation is not inherently sinful. Plato, however, taught that the body, for example, is a distraction. It detracts us from the pure exercise of reason.

But according to the Bible, there are a couple of big problems here. In the first place, it's sin that's bad, not the body. In the second place, man's reason is no less depraved than his body. So, reason is not "pure," and the body is not inherently bad. Both reason and the body in every aspect of man are subject to sin in his sinful state, but all of them can be redeemed.

Escapism

And if the material world is inherently bad, there's no reason we need to work to redeem it. This is where a dangerous form of pietism entered the church very early. The monastics and the Desert Fathers retreated from this present physical world and, as good Christian neo-Platonists, tried to escape it.[19] They did not claim the material world for Christ the King. They were escapists, not reclaimers.

Today, we see this in much of Dispensationalism[20] and the

House, 1971), 93-94.
19. "Monasticism," in ed., Jerald C. Brauer, *The Westminster Dictionary of Church History* (Philadelphia: Westminster, 1971), 563.
20. For a theological refutation, see Oswald T. Allis, *Prophecy and the Church* (Phillipsburg, New Jersey: Presbyterian and Reformed, 1978).

"Left Behind" series. Tim LaHaye is well meaning, but I believe he is very, very wrong. His leading views are much more Greek than Christian at this point. We do not live to escape the world. We live to obey God and to press His claims in every area of life and thought. The Christian Platonists, however, want an escape, and not victory. This is because they tend to view the material world and the human body as inherently restrictive.

I recently encountered one of the most flagrant examples of this I've ever read. Listen to these staggering words from St. Gregory the Theologian, Archbishop of Constantinople:

> For, nothing seems to be so desirable as to close the doors of my senses, and escaping from the flesh and the world, having no involvement in human affairs beyond what is absolutely necessary, and conversing with myself and with God, to live above the level of visible saints, always preserving within myself the Divine reflections pure and unmixed with the unstable impressions of the world below, both being and ever becoming like a spotless mirror of God and of Divine things, acquiring light by means of light and the clearer by means of the obscurer, until I reach the source of the effulgence which we enjoy here and attain to my blessed goal, once the mirrors have been destroyed by the truth; for, it is only with difficulty that anyone, either by educating himself with a long course of philosophy, gradually separating the noble and luminous parts of the soul from that which is debase and yoked with darkness, or by gaining the mercy of God, or by both of these together, and by making it a habit to look upward as much as possible, can prevail over matter, which always drags us down.[21]

This is by a Byzantine (Greek) theologian, and it is Platonic to the core. Plato could have said "Amen" to virtually everything that this theologian uttered!

This is a theology in life that escapes. The present world is

---

21. Saint Gregory the Theologian, "An Oration on the Nature of Christian Doctrine," *Orthodox Tradition*, Vol. 20, No. 2 [2003], 26.

bad, the body is bad, material things are bad — so I must turn my mind away from them if I am to please God.

This is a denial of God's sovereignty over all areas of life and thought; it is the denial of the goodness of God's created order; it is a denial of the Lordship of Christ over all things.

Deprecation of the Resurrection

But there is something even more dangerous about this Christian Platonism and classical view of Christianity. If it devalues the human body, then it must discount the doctrine of the resurrection, which is all about the body. This is where it gets into its worst trouble. The doctrine of the resurrection is probably the central doctrine of the entire Bible.[22] Christ not only died, but He rose again, ascending into Heaven to become Lord over all things. The resurrection of Jesus creates the new birth in repentant sinners and energizes the church and Christians and is the force pushing Christianity throughout the world.

But in recent years we have lost the significance of this doctrine. We have lost it largely through Platonizing tendencies in the church. For example, at Christian funerals, how often do we hear the precious doctrine of the resurrection mentioned? Rather, we only hear about the decedent's dying and going to Heaven. It is a doctrine of escape. The body perishes, but the soul is immortal; it flies up to the Christian version of the Forms and Ideas — some sort of ethereal Heaven. The doctrine of the resurrection is thereby de-emphasized.

But in the Bible, our blessed future is not simply to fly around Heaven as soulful beings. Rather, it is to live in resurrected bodies on a renovated earth. Note carefully what Revelation 21 tells us — in the eternal state (if we can even use that language) we do not go up to Heaven to dwell with God. Rather, John tells us, the New Jerusalem comes down to earth (a renovated earth), and God dwells with us.[23] It's all very "materialistic."

---

22. Daniel P. Fuller, *Easter Faith and History* (Grand Rapids: Eerdmans, 1965), 19.
23. N. T. Wright, *Surprised By Hope* (New York: HarperOne, 2008).

Plato invites us to escape the material world; God invites us to *relish* the material world — the world that He has created, and the world that He is redeeming. Note this carefully. The Bible says flatly that God alone is immortal (1 Tim. 6:16). He brings immortality to light by the Gospel (2 Tim. 1:10). Men do not have preexistent, immortal souls. Now, those who trust in Christ are perhaps granted the *seed* of immortality in the Holy Spirit when they are united to Christ, but they *gain* immortality only in the resurrection. Paul says this plainly in 1 Corinthians 15 — this mortal shall put on immortality (v. 54). If you put it on, that means you didn't have it before! We live forever not as some sort of "soulish" being, but as a resurrected individual, made in the image of God. (Unbelievers, too, will be resurrected, and they will be judged.)

When we die, we don't cease to exist ("soul sleep"); however, the Bible does not say in what *form* we exist. At death, we're no longer full beings, because we lack a body. We are only full individuals when we possess a body. This is why the resurrection is so important. *The Christian is not fully redeemed until he is resurrected.* Before that, death still has power over him.

But perhaps the most staggering, exciting, overwhelming statement about the glories of the resurrection in contrast with the static Greek view of the immortality of the soul was set forth in the classic statement by Oscar Cullmann:

> The death of Socrates is a beautiful death. Nothing is seen here of death's terror. Socrates cannot fear death, since indeed it sets us free from the body. Whoever fears death proves that he loves the world of the body, that he is thoroughly entangled in the world of the senses. Death is the soul's great friend. So he teaches; and so, in wonderful harmony with his teaching, he dies — this man who embodied the Greek world in its noblest form.

> And now let us hear how Jesus dies. In Gethsemane he knows that death stands before him, just as Socrates expected death on his last day. The synoptic evangelists furnish us, by and large, with a unanimous report. Jesus begins "to tremble and be distressed," writes Mark. "My soul is troubled, even

to death," he says to his disciples. Jesus is so thoroughly human that he shares the natural fear of death. Jesus is afraid ... He is afraid in the face of death itself. Death for him is not something divine; it is something dreadful.

[...]

Only he who apprehends with the first Christians the horror of death, who takes death seriously as death, can comprehend the Easter exultation of the primitive Christian community and understand that the whole thinking of the New Testament is governed by belief in the resurrection. Belief in the immortality of the soul is not belief in a revolutionary event. Immortality, in fact, is only a *negative* assertion: the soul does *not* die, but simply lives on. Resurrection is a *positive* assertion: the whole man, who has really died, is recalled to life by a new act of creation by God. Something has happened — a miracle of creation! For something has also happened previously, something fearful: life formed by God has been destroyed.

Death in itself is not beautiful, not even the death of Jesus. Death before Easter is really the death's head surrounded by the odor of decay. And the death of Jesus is as loathsome as the great painter Grünewald depicted it in the Middle Ages. But precisely for this reason the same painter understood how to paint, along with it, in an incomparable way, the great victory, the resurrection of Christ... Whoever paints a pretty death can paint no resurrection. Whoever has not grasped the horror of death cannot join Paul in the hymn of victory: "Death is swallowed up — in victory! O death, where is thy victory? O death, where is thy sting?"[24]

So deeply has classicism influenced Christianity that some Christians would think this quote strange. So deeply has Platonism influenced Christianity that at times we despair to find the true Faith.

---

24. Oscar Cullmann, "Immortality of the Soul or Resurrection of the Dead," in ed., Krister Stendahl, *Immortality and Resurrection* (New York: MacMillan, 1965), 9-53.

Conclusion

Biblical Faith is about a Sovereign God ruling all things by means of His Son, Jesus Christ, Lord of Heaven and earth. He is a very *physical* Son, and He died a *physical* death, and rose *physically* from the grave. He now rules all things, not just "spiritual" things. There is no world of the Forms and Ideas. This is just an absurd, pagan speculation — whether undertaken by Plato or Christians influenced by him. There is no "ideal world." There is only the world under Christ's authority. The hope of man is not a soulish escape from this life, when the body is cracked as a walnut shell and the fruit inside gains liberation. No! Man made in God's image has both material and immaterial parts, but *both* are needed. At death, man becomes less than a full individual. For the Christian, only at the resurrection will he become again a full being, this time fully sanctified.

Platonism, Christian Platonism, and classical philosophy constitute a world of godless rationalism, contempt for the created order, and a lust for escape.

Christianity is founded on Faith, not reason; it enjoys and wishes to redeem the material world; and it looks not for escape — it looks for victory under Christ's authority.[25] We can be Christians, or we can be classicists.

We cannot be both.

---

5. John Jefferson Davis, *Christ's Victorious Kingdom* (Grand Rapids: Baker, 1986).

CHAPTER 10

Adult Children, Childish Adults

This is the high end toward which all Christian training must be directed [:]

In holy Baptism to receive the mark of this King, and, soon as consciousness wakens, to acquaint the child with that King, as with a King Who bears rule eternally, Who also must bear rule over him, and to Whom likewise every child given us of God in His favor, owes submission as subject, and the tribute of praise and worship.

So only do you come to the generation-idea of faith.

Abraham Kuyper, *When Thou Sittest in Thine House*[1]

The topic of our precise relationship to adult children enjoys very little treatment in the Bible. There are issues that exercise us in this life for which we wish there were extensive Biblical revelation, but we must be careful not to invent it when it's not there. The silences of the Bible are as awesome as the statements. In fact, if God didn't include revelation about some topic, we might conclude that He didn't want us to have ironclad certainty about it, and these silences may annoy those of us who covet certainty at all costs.[2] This is true about issues like baptism and space travel and music standards. And it really becomes thorny on matters of ethics — right and wrong. What about activities that we dislike but which the Bible does not mention, let alone prohibit, like smoking cigarettes or getting tattoos or listening to the Rolling Stones? We can always flee to the "good and necessary" clause

---

1. (Grand Rapids: Eerdmans, 1929), 394.
2. A. Berkeley Michelson and Alvera M. Michelson, *Understanding Scripture* (Peabody, Massachusetts: Hendrickson, 1982, 1992), 125.

of the Westminster Confession of Faith, yet we should recall that many conclusions are good, but not necessary (vacations), and others are necessary, but not good (war). What about ethics in matters beyond Scripture?

We could always invoke natural revelation. This is what Hitler did in arguing for the superiority of the German race — nature itself teaches us that the Aryan race is God's chosen. Natural revelation easily becomes a wax nose. The godly person can derive ethics from natural revelation, but most are not godly; and in any case, that revelation doesn't provide the specific answers we so desperately want.[3]

How do we know what is right and wrong with certainty?

If we really affirm Biblical authority,[4] and give it more than lip service, we might follow an operative dictum that *whatever the Bible does not forbid, God permits.*[5] This is a theoretical way of saying that only God can define sin (1 Jn. 3:4). When somebody charges that to advocate birth control or smoking tobacco or charging interest is *ipso facto* sin, he has replaced God's law with man's law. This is a mark of Pharisees (Mk. 7:1-16). **Only God is entitled to define sin**.

It's true that there may be many good reasons not to practice birth control, smoke cigars, charge interest, grow huckleberries, listen to the Beatles, drink single-malt scotch, dance at weddings, drive a convertible, send your daughter to Ivy League colleges, sport Afros, invest in mutual funds, play slots in Las Vegas, watch R-rated movies, learn to whittle, or wear linen sport coats — but none of those reasons have any inherent bearing on sin. If you cannot practice these things in good conscience, then don't practice them (Rom. 14:23). Just don't criticize Christians who do practice them.

---

3. G. C. Berkouwer, *General Revelation* (Grand Rapids: Eerdmans, 1955), ch. 7.

4. Arguably the most incisive restatement of the orthodox view of Biblical authority written in the last 100 years is Clark H. Pinnock, *Biblical Revelation* (Chicago: Moody, 1971). His more recent adoption of deviant views like "Open Theism" should not distract us from his earlier, stalwart work.

5. R. J. Rushdoony, "Inferences and Commandments," *Roots of Reconstruction* (Vallecito, California: Ross House, 1991), 434-436.

The reason this issue is important, in fact, has nothing to do with cigar smoking and interest charging and U2 albums, and everything to do with the functional authority and integrity of the Bible. God has laid out what He requires. Beyond what He requires, He grants freedom: we term this "Christian liberty." We could use a revival of it today. Bible-toters and -quoters who forbid what the Bible does not address dilute the authority of the Bible, a serious matter indeed.

The Bible (of course) does not address all issues, and we have civil and ecclesiastical and parental authorities that (when necessary, but only when necessary) fill in the legislative lacuna: citizens may not jay walk, members must attend church at 11:00 a.m. and not 3 in the afternoon, and people may not try alcohol publicly until they are 21.

But these, let it always be understood, are men's permissible laws, not God's prescriptive laws.

We have enough sin around today (homosexuality, slander, abortion, love-lessness, schism, drunkenness, covenant-breaking, unbelief, worry, statism) that we need not add to the list birth control, smoking, and full-bodied merlots.

The bottom line is: *Only God gets to define sin.* We may not impinge on His sovereignty.

So, in pondering our relationship to our adult children, let's try to be dogmatic where the Bible is dogmatic and be flexible where the Bible is silent.

With that proviso in mind, I'll offer four theses for your consideration.

Thesis # 1. ***Because the Bible has almost nothing to say about the relationship between parents and unmarried adult children, Biblical wisdom must prevail.***

Have you ever considered the role that the book of Proverbs may play in the formation of Biblical ethics? If all ethics could be derived from Biblical propositions, why would we need wisdom? We could merely read all our ethical decisions right out of the Bible or at least derive them logically from the Bible (here's the scholastic [non-Biblical] language again — "good and necessary consequence").

But if the Bible is *not* an inexhaustible supply of ethical propositions, we might actually need wisdom. We might need to pray and cry out to God. To consult with our family and friends and elders. To examine common-sense conclusions from history. In other words, all that we need to know about ethics is *not* in the Bible. If it were, we would never need the wisdom required by the Book of Proverbs.

Does this thesis conflict with what I said about permitting what the Bible doesn't prohibit? No, it doesn't. Wisdom (for example) may dictate that you *not* finance your daughter's college education since she needs to pay for it, but wisdom is not identical to revelation. You and I may not impose this wise decision on everybody else. Wisdom may be defined as knowing what to do in a very concrete situation with very specific people. It may not apply to everybody else in every similar situation. Is this a Biblical form of situation ethics? Yes, it is. Is it always wrong to kill? No, it's not. You may kill in warfare. Is it always *right* to pray? No, it is not — if prayer is an excuse for godly action.

Similarly, it may be wise for you to encourage your 18-year-old daughter to live with some responsible girlfriends, but that doesn't mean *every* other mother or father should do this. Wisdom is not designed to be imposed on all but embraced in specific, concrete circumstances.

And how do we get that wisdom? When we need guidance on where to suggest our children attend college, or whom they should marry, or whether they should date or "court" or practice some combination of the two or what "version" of dating or courtship, or whether you should help them financially and if so how much, or whether you should offer marital advice or just keep your big trap shut, where should we turn?

James 1 tells us that God will grant wisdom to us if we ask in faith. But many of us never ask God. We'd rather read copiously and ascertain a "logical" answer. We might think that prayer could lead to a "subjective" answer that could not be verified propositionally. Of course, it couldn't. That's why we need to pray in the first place.

How rarely we — I — cry out to God for wisdom. No wonder we commit such stupid blunders. We think we'll simply "do the right thing" by intuition, without consistently seeking God's face for wisdom in dealing with our adult children.

Then, of course, we get wisdom from the Word, though not just in an inductive, propositional sense. In other words, not just looking for answers to our questions.

No, the wisdom literature reshapes *us* and we become wise as we live and walk within the sphere of God's Word. Tom Wright is mistaken, I think, to assume that this is the chief meaning of Biblical authority (in his book *The Last Word*), but he *is* onto something.[6]

When George Bush was running for the Presidency in 2000, Barbara Walters asked him how his faith would shape his political policies. He answered, "My Christian Faith won't shape my political policies, but it will shape *me*."

That wasn't the precisely correct answer, but it was partly correct. The Bible isn't a propositional textbook. It's a lamp and light, and it's food that sustains us and changes us.

So, when we read the Word, we don't read it only for answers. We read it as the living word that changes us (Heb. 4:12). And in changing us, it makes us wise.

In other words, if we are versed in wise revelation, we'll tend to *reflexively* make wise choices.

When you're with your adult son and he makes a questionable suggestion, there may not be time to look at your Bible — in fact, there may not be an applicable Bible verse at all. But you'll likely give wise advice to him if the wisdom of the Bible has shaped your thinking and character — not just given you an answer to a specific ethical question.

So, if you wish to know how to treat adult children, get wisdom; the propositions of the Bible won't give you most of the answers.

---

6. See my review: "The Bible and the Big Story: The Bibliological Burden of N. T. Wright," *Act 3 Review*, Vol. 15, No. 2 [2006], 129-139.

Thesis # 2. ***Marriage creates a new covenant; the spouses enter a new bond and different relationship to their previous family.***

We read at the very beginning of Scripture that the man must leave his father and mother and cleave to his wife and they two will be one (Gen. 2:24). This creates a radically new covenant relationship with two new people. The old relationship isn't gone, but it is transformed. A married son's relationship to his parents is not the same as that of an unmarried son (just as an adult unmarried son's relationship to his parents is not the same as a son growing up in his parents' house).

There is linguistic ambiguity sometimes. At times my wife and I exhibit that ambiguity. I'll ask her, "Are you going back to visit your family this fall?" And she'll reply, "My family is *here*." But the same is true of the husband. When you get married, you have *your* family as well as the family in which you were reared — your father and mother's family.

It's hard to overemphasize the fact that this really is a *new* relationship. When a man and a woman — your son or daughter — marries, they sustain an altered covenantal relation to you. The relationship changes, and therefore *we* as the parents must change.

One of my sons had a close relationship with a fine young lady. She needed to pay off her college loans, and she needed to move to another part of the country to get a job to do that. He can't move. Now, as I told him, if he were married, the situation would be different. She would be obliged to stay with him. And he with her. But they are not married, and she's not obliged to stay with him. There is no covenant bond and, thus, no covenant obligation.

By the way, this new marriage covenant entails new obligations. From the parental side, those obligations lessen considerably. They may have lessened earlier with adult children who have left your home, but they surely lessen with marriage. The responsibility of a parent to adult children seems to be chiefly prayer and love and encouragement. It is not teaching or provision. Men, you're not obliged to support your adult son or daughter, much less your married son or daughter.

2 Corinthians 12:14 states that the parents should lay up [wealth] for the children, not the obverse. So, parents should save money or possessions for their children and give them at some point as an inheritance to godly (not ungodly) children. You should plan for doing this — if nothing else, in the equity of your home.

But you're not required to meet their every need. In fact, doing this can be positively harmful. You might be teaching them that it doesn't matter if they make imprudent financial decisions, good ole sugar daddy will always bail them out. Don't insulate your adult children from the consequences of their bad decisions.

One of my sons (I won't tell you which one) likes fast, cool cars. I also won't tell you where he picked up that trait. His mother isn't here to defend herself. Anyway, one morning years ago he came into my room sheepishly and told me he'd gotten a ticket while driving my convertible the night before.

"Well, OK, you can pay it," I responded. "How fast were you going."

He was still sheepish. "Hmm. Well, Peter and I were drag racing."

Hmmm. I called the Mariposa County Courthouse to find out the fine for (ready?) "engaging in a speed contest."

"Sir, that fine is $500-1000." So, I told my son he'd have to pay it. I wasn't going to pay it for him. I could have mitigated the consequences of his bad decision. It would have been the easy thing for me to do and the easy thing for him.

The easy thing, but not the right thing.

Don't insulate your adult children from the consequences of their bad decisions.

And you are not obliged to give them advice. They may be encouraged to solicit that advice, but you are not obligated to give it.

You are there to pray and love and support, but not dictate terms.

And beware of the temptation to interfere at those inevitable difficult times. That's when it's most necessary that you not interfere. Short of abuse or adultery or abandonment or apostasy, parents, steer your daughter back to her husband and tell them to work things about. Never offer an easy way for your married children to separate or "come back home." They have their own new home. They made their bed, and they need to sleep in it — literally.

Marriage, I submit, creates a new covenant; the spouses enter a new bond and different relationship to their previous family.

Thesis # 3 — *Children are commanded to honor their parents for a lifetime, but the command to obey does not seem to extend to a lifetime.*

Let me tell you why. The wife is called to submit to her husband, but if the husband is required to obey his father and mother, then the wife must ultimately submit to them, not her husband. There is no warrant in the Bible for such an arrangement. The wife must submit to her husband, not some other man, not even her father-in-law. And woe be to any wife who allows her husband to submit to his father. This is a recipe for disaster.

Immediately someone will point out that Israel was a patriarchal society, and that a son and daughters-in-law often lived near their parents; but that fact is descriptive, not prescriptive. This is an important hermeneutical distinction in applying Biblical ethics.[7] **The fact that something is described doesn't mean it's *normative*.** We must carefully distinguish the descriptive from the prescriptive dimensions of the Bible.

For example, we think of Jephthah and his daughter. Should we follow his example and keep our vows even if it means murdering our daughter?

How about a snazzy way to get a daughter-in-law, men. Send one of your long-time employees into a foreign country and bring back a wife for your son? How about promising that if God

---

7. Gordon J. Wenham, "Family in the Pentateuch," in eds., Richard S. Hess and M. Daniel Carroll R. [*sic*], *Family in the Bible* (Grand Rapids: Baker, 2003), 30-31.

gives you a son, you'll leave him to live at the church for the elders to rear when he's about four or five years old (Samuel)?

These are all descriptive events, not prescriptive events. They're given to us so that we can learn some lesson but not that we should mimic them (Rom. 15:4).[8]

So, the fact that nearly all the ancient cultures were patriarchal doesn't mean that we are required to be patriarchal, any more than the fact that nearly all the ancient cultures were agrarian means that we must all raise chickens and huckleberries for a living. In an agrarian and patriarchal culture, all of Jacob's sons seemed to live right near him. The Bible *permits* this style of living (like the Amish), but it doesn't require it. Similarly, the Levites and priests in the old covenant economy were tribal — son followed father in the spiritual vocation. But the Bible doesn't command that elders' sons, and nobody else, be elders — there is no required patriarchal line in church leadership.

Now, I bring this up simply to say that ancient social patterns are not normative; only prescriptive revelation is normative. How do we adults honor our parents?

Jesus makes plain that by supporting them financially, we honor them (Mk. 7). There is a tenderness and concern between parents and children in this care. When Jesus was about to be crucified he commanded that Mary be John the apostle's mother and John be her son; John then took her into his home to care for her.

We honor our older parents by providing for them. You young sons need to plan now to care for your parents in their old age. Preferably that would be in your own home. In some cases, this is not possible, but in any case, this seems to be a clear Biblical requirement of honoring your parents — and maybe the chief one.

But must a daughter obey her parents all her days? It seems not. She is called to submit to her husband, not her father if she's married (I'll get to unmarried, adult daughters next). Daughters, if you constantly compare your father to your husband, if you

8. Henry A. Virkler, *Hermeneutics* (Grand Rapids: Baker, 1981), 212-223.

pine for "home" (meaning your father's home rather than yours), if you try to manipulate your husband to live near your parents rather than follow where God has called him, you are deviating from Biblical precept.

By the way, young ladies, this is why you had better check out that young buckaroo before you marry him. In marrying a man, you're marrying his leadership, his vision, his abilities, his dreams, his calling. You are called by God to assist him in this calling. If you can't support or abide that calling, you'd better send him a Dear John letter. You can't separate a man from his calling. So, know this man's calling and decide whether you can submit to that calling and support it.

But must a *son* obey his parents all his days? Again, it seems not. Ephesians 5 and 1 Corinthians 7 make clear that a man's life is largely wrapped up in his wife, in love and provision and sacrifice. This dedication seems clearly in conflict with the command to obey one's parents in the Lord at all times. You can't do both. That's why the command to leave father and mother in creating a new marital covenant seems to imply a revision in the command to obey your parents. You honor them, but you are not required to obey.

And of course, godly parents would never demand such obedience. They know that the son or daughter has joined a *new* covenant; the old covenant relationship is gone forever.

Sons, if it means moving to New Zealand to protect your family from parental meddling, you need to start packing. It's that serious.

Several months ago a dear friend of mine, a young man about 27, came to me and the other elders at our church home. His father is a spiritual autocrat — the latest episode went like this. This young family had their first child, and during labor the wife (a godly and modest young woman) asked that everybody leave the room except the doctor while she delivered the baby. My friend's father was there and was ushered out of the room and was irate. He later wrote a screed to his son reprimanding him and his daughter-in-law for their refusal to take advice and share their life with their "superiors" and claimed that if they did not change God's judgment would fall on them. And my description here has only touched the surface — the letter was filled with arrogance and autocracy and manipulation all wrapped up in the most spiritual language — a real Pharisaic winner.

This letter was just crushing to the young wife. Her husband, my long-time friend, told me, "I've put up with this for 27 years, so maybe I should just let this go and not say anything."

We responded, "Don't you *dare* do that. You may be able to get away with suffering tyranny yourself, but you have no right to subject your wife and new child to it. Your relationship to your parents has changed. Tell your Dad that unless he apologizes and repents, he'll never see your wife and his grandchild again."

And he hasn't. And he may *never* see them if he doesn't repent and mend his autocratic ways.

Of course, this is an extreme case. One hopes and prays that it never happens to any of you. But the husband is called to protect his family from such interference, no matter what its source.

And, parents, *respect that new covenant.* Love your adult children and encourage them. But respect the newness of the new marital covenant.

Repeat: children are commanded to honor their parents for a lifetime, but the command to obey does not seem to extend to a lifetime.

Thesis # 4 — ***Adult, unmarried sons and daughters are not subject to the authority of their parents merely on the grounds that they are not yet married.***

This thesis is more tenuous since the Bible says almost nothing about unmarried adult children. We know that widows should be cared for by family members if they are not yet 60 years old (1 Tim. 5). We know from 1 Corinthians 7 that singlehood is preferable,[9] but there is no indication of parental interference in the decision to marry. If parents have authority over married

---

9. Richard B. Hays, *1 Corinthians* (Louisville, Kentucky: John Knox, 1997), 132-133.

adult children, it would seem that there would be at least a hint of this in 1 Corinthians 7, but there is none.

Of course, it's assumed that parents even of unmarried adults (not to mention the church) are always there, praying and encouraging and loving. But the real question is parental *authority*, not parental involvement. Are single 20-year-olds subject to the authority of their parents? If we say yes, we'd need to explain if single 50-year-olds are subject to the authority of their parents, and if not, why not? Is the issue financial support? If the adult child is financially dependent, is he subject to his parents, but if he is financially independent, is he no longer subject? This is likely a scenario the Bible does not envision.

We traditionally have the father "give away" the daughter in the marriage ceremony. This act is symbolically saying, "I'm trans-ferring my daughter from my family to the groom's (new) family." If the father is dead or an unbeliever, often an older brother or friend assumes this role. At that point, the issue is not so much the transfer of authority, but simply a show of endorsement: "I agree with this marriage," he's saying.

Of course, the Bible doesn't require this act of "covenant transfer," or even mention it, so nobody's conscience could be bound to it. Marriage ceremonies are not a matter of Biblical ethics.

Nor is there any Biblical distinction between unmarried adult sons and unmarried adult daughters. We sometimes act as though daughters are bound to obey their parents as long as they're not married, while unmarried adult sons sort of drift into their own authority structure over time. But the Bible makes no such distinc-tion. What is true of daughters is apparently also true of sons.

The father can rescind a daughter's vow if she is "young and in her father's house" (Num. 30), but how young is young, and is she required to live in her father's house until she's married? The Bible just doesn't say. In ancient patriarchal cultures, a woman likely stayed in her father's house until she was married, but patri-archal cultures are an accident of history, not prescriptive Biblical ethics.

If children are not commanded to obey their parents for their entire lives, at what point are they no longer subject to parental authority?

Some might say 20 years old, since that's the age at which each Jew was taxed for the sanctuary (Ex. 30), and in Numbers 1 we discover that was the age at which men go to war. But it's not clear that these acts are related to liberation from parental authority.

Legally in the West, a person becomes an adult at 18 years old, and according to Romans 13, we must honor the state unless it prohibits what the Bible requires or requires what the Bible prohibits. It may not be the best answer, but it's at present the legal answer.

It's here (I believe) that Biblical wisdom, not propositional revelation, must govern. Some 16-year-olds are ready to leave parental authority (many godly young women have gotten married at that age). Conversely, some 30-year-old young men aren't ready to leave parental authority. They have never learned submission and self-reliance and self-discipline and so on. In the words of Mark Driscoll, these young theonomists talk about taking dominion over the world, but they can't even take dominion over their own messy bedroom.

Of course, legally all of this is moot since our society arbitrarily has established 18 years old as the point of adulthood.

To you older children, I say, honor your parents all the days of your life. That command persists for a lifetime. But how do you know when to "leave home"? Seek the Lord's face. Talk candidly with your parents and your elders and your godly friends.

Parents, don't cling to your children. A friend from Virginia called me, an elder in a Reformed church there. His daughter's friend is an unmarried 25-year-old woman. Her father had fallen into the patriarchical ideology and was pushy and demanding. She wanted to move out of his house for the sake of her own sanity, and she prayed and discussed the matter with my friend and with her pastor, who supported her in this decision. She wasn't a rebel. She wasn't a troublemaker. She just needed to get away from the suppression and suffocation of her father. In my view the pastor and elders were correct to advise her as they did. She's now living in another state and doing just fine.

She didn't make this decision on her own but obtained godly counsel. This is the right tack — for unmarried adult daughters or unmarried adult sons.

A final word: The most subtle encouragement and expression of love to our adult children are exponentially more effective than the most ringing rebuke. Even in exasperating circumstances, it's amazing how love prevails.

Twenty-five years ago a friend uttered a statement to me I'll never forget. "If according to 1 Corinthians 13 love *never* fails, why do we use anything else?"

It's a dictum to ponder in our relationships to our adult children.[10]

---

10. I judge the most incisive and informative Christian volume on child training in English to be Andrew Murray, *How to Raise Your Children for Christ* (Minneapolis: Bethany House, 1975).